SUSAN LAWRENCE: IN THE WRIGHT HOUSE

SUSAN LAWRENCE: THE ENIGMA IN THE WRIGHT HOUSE

BY

ROBERTA VOLKMANN

www.bookstandpublishing.com

Published by
Bookstand Publishing
Morgan Hill, CA 95037
3379_4

ISBN 978-1-58909-960-9

Printed in the United States of America

ACKNOWLEDGEMENTS

This book is the culmination of the efforts of three groups of people on whose work I built and to whom I am deeply grateful.

- The Gatherers of history: Researchers: David Diederich, Donald Hallmark, Nancy Long, Regina McGuire, and Kim Perez; those who conducted oral histories years ago; and those who were willing to share their memories with me: R Lou Barker, Joan Smith, and Audrey Vieau.
- The Guardians of history: Mark Johnson, Illinois Historic Preservation Agency; Cindy Luton, Unity Church; the staffs at the Abraham Lincoln Presidential Library, the Dana-Thomas House and Foundation, and the Sangamon Valley Collection in Lincoln Library, Springfield's public library.
- The Reviewers of my work: Corrine Frisch, Ann Heelan, Donald Hoffmann, and my ever-patient and meticulous husband, Carl Volkmann.

One man played all of those roles. As a Gatherer, Guardian, and Reviewer, Dr. Richard Taylor was indispensable in the development of this project. For his meticulous research, wise counsel, and generous spirit, I am indebted and dedicate Susan's biography to him.

INTRODUCTION

"Who was Susan Lawrence Dana?" The volunteer interpreter had heard that question time and time again as she led tourists through the 35 room Frank Lloyd Wright designed Dana-Thomas House. This tour group had stood in awe in the reception hall, the dining room, and the gallery, all two-story social spaces. They had walked through the library, the duck pin alley, and the master bedroom. They had peeked into the three other bedroom suites. The interpreter had pointed out the three original works of art that Wright had incorporated into the design of the house: George Niedecken's mural that surrounded the guests in the dining room and two original sculptures by Richard Bock. More than 100 pieces of furniture, 250 leaded glass windows and doors, and over 100 art glass fixtures designed by Wright over 100 years ago had overwhelmed the tourists. When the young man asked the interpreter the inevitable question about the woman who commissioned Wright's design, the interpreter could have repeated descriptions of Susan Lawrence Dana used by reporters and authors over the years: beautiful, charming, brilliant, colorful, eccentric, willful, capricious, wealthy, social, or artistic. However, Susan was much more. Born in 1862, Susan Lawrence Dana lived during a period in history when women were finding their voices and carving out new roles in society. As the world changed around her, she assumed several names and played many roles. Over her lifetime Susan developed a complex, independent lifestyle that could not be captured in a few words. The interpreter answered the tourist with her usual response to that question: "It would take a book to discover the enigma that was Susan Lawrence."

Table of Contents

1

SUE C. LAWRENCE (SUSIE, TAG, LITTLE RHEUNA): DAUGHTER

It's a girl! Rheuna and Mary Lawrence were elated! Still grieving for their first daughter Agnes Salome who had died less than two years earlier when she was just 11 months old, the young couple welcomed a new life to nurture and to love. Grandma Lawrence, who had been living with her son's family since Agnes Salome's death, had special reason to rejoice. Rheuna and Mary chose to name their new daughter Sue C., a variation of Susan, Grandma Lawrence's given name. Although her parents later expanded the C to Caroline, from her birth on October 13, 1862, the little girl was called Susie.[1]

Rheuna and Mary were just beginning their life together. Born in Ohio, twenty-five year old Rheuna had come to Springfield, Illinois, by way of Chicago about five years earlier. He had married Mary Agnes Maxcy, daughter of early Springfield settlers John and Farnetta Maxcy, on January 24, 1859, when he was 22 and she was 17. Rheuna began his diverse career in the young city's burgeoning building industry as a mason. Soon he was supporting his young family as a building contractor, a grocer, and a Union Army supplier.

Rheuna Lawrence was an intuitive entrepreneur and an astute opportunist. Over the years his business instincts served him well as his wealth grew through investments in such ventures as real estate, railroad construction, and coal mine development. His most successful endeavors were his gold and silver mines in Colorado and Oregon. While he was building his material assets, he was cultivating friendships with powerful people including governors. These connections led to numerous appointments to local, state, and national boards and commissions. As an active Republican, he was elected to one term as mayor of Springfield and appointed to the Springfield School Board which he chaired for several years. In 1898 the street on which Rheuna's home stood was changed from Wright Street to Lawrence Avenue, presumably to honor him. Additionally, Rheuna was an active Mason, a volunteer fireman, and the president of the State National Bank.

As Rheuna's fortune and reputation grew, he and Mary remained unpretentious. Contrary to the stereotype of the *nou-veau riche*, the couple continued to be grounded in the core values of their humble beginnings. They shared a strong work ethic and a commitment to serve others in their community. An anonymous biographer of Rheuna described him in this way:

> He used and enjoyed costly things, but, in the main, lived simply, while he abhorred ostentation and disliked an expenditure on luxuries which was all out of proportion to any real enjoyment he got from them. [and] He deplored the tendency among many rich people to consume on expensive domestic establishments the entire income of great properties.[2]

Rheuna did, however, indulge in one public manifestation of his newly acquired wealth. Six years after Susie's birth he bought the lot on the corner of Fourth and Wright Streets in the neighborhood that was called "Aristocracy Hill." There he built a tasteful 13 room brick Italianate-style home for his immediate and extended family which was always changing. Rheuna's mother and Mary's mother Farnetta Maxcy each spent her last years in the home. One extended family member, Florence Cliffen Lawrence, who was the daughter of Rheuna's brother, was a permanent resident. Nine years older than Susie, "Cousin Flora" joined the household when Susie was 10 years old and lived with the family for more than 55 years.

Much of Mary's time and energy was spent on clubs and charitable activities, and she took her projects seriously. Her involvement with the Lincoln Colored Home exemplifies her values and leadership skills. The home was founded by Eva Monroe, an African-American woman who had saved enough of her own money for a down-payment on an old house which she opened for African-American orphaned children and elderly women in 1898. To keep her doors open, she solicited money and materials from both the white and black Springfield community. Mary Lawrence came to her aid. Mary assumed the $1,400 mortgage on the house. Later she acquired the deed to the property so that the old house could be razed and a new one built. She supervised the design of the new home and donated windows, doors, and chandeliers from her own former home. During the building process, the 37 residents and staff lived in tents with no water. Mary Lawrence arranged city water service to the property. In addition to her many personal contributions, she organized fund raisers, enlisted local business leaders for service on the board of directors, and obtained annual funding from the county for the home.

After Mary's death, the building was dedicated as a memorial to her. In May 1906 Susie transferred the deed clear of all indebtedness to the board of directors with the stipulation that the building would be used for its original purpose or be returned to Susie.[3] Mary Lawrence continued to be remembered in the Springfield African-American community. In 1915 Eva Monroe opened the Mary Lawrence Industrial School for Girls, and the Mary A. Lawrence Woman's Club was organized by a group of African-American women.[4] For many reasons the Lincoln Colored Home continued to struggle financially, and due to a number of societal changes and legal difficulties, the doors closed in 1933.

Mary Agnes Lawrence
Dana-Thomas House Archives

15 Year Old Susie Lawrence
Dana-Thomas House Archives

Susie was the center of the busy life of Rheuna and Mary. She was especially close to her father. He called her "Tag." Observing the close relationship, friends of the family dubbed her "Little Rheuna."

Susie's only formal education of record was at ages seven and eight when she attended the Bettie Stuart Institute located just down the street from the Lawrence residence on Fourth Street near the Governor's Mansion. The Institute Catalogue defined the "thorough and efficient" curriculum offered at the school. It included reading, writing, spelling, mental arithmetic, object lessons, primary geography, Child's Book of Nature, drawing, and gymnastics. Among Susie's classmates were Leigh Gross, a close friend into adulthood, and Charles Gehrmann, the man who would become her third husband.[5]

Although it is possible that Susie had further formal education, no record has been found of her attendance in any other school. Some evidence suggests that she was a student at Mrs. J. F. Brooks' School for Young Ladies at 617 South Fifth Street. The school was run by the second wife of Reverend J. F. Brooks, a renowned educator who had established a female seminary with a progressive curriculum including drawing, painting, and music at that address in 1849. The school was closed four years later when Brooks' first wife died. Her sister became his second wife and re-opened the academy. With her husband's assistance, she offered an expanded curriculum to many of Susie's contemporaries.[6]

To assure that their only daughter was exposed to the finer things in life, Rheuna and Mary provided her with instruction in art, music, and even roller skating. The local newspapers reported that at age 14 Susie performed "Echo of Lucerne" in a piano recital "with the precision of a Swiss music box"[7] and won the lady's gold medal prize at the Springfield Roller Skating Association.[8] Miss Susie Lawrence exhibited a plush mirror frame in an art show of the students of Miss May Lee, a resident of New York who came to Springfield to give art lessons to the community at Mrs. Brooks' school.[9]

On February 7, 1879, the house on Fourth and Wright Streets was lit up as it had never been before. Although they rarely entertained on a large scale, Rheuna and Mary were proudly hosting *Qui Vive,* a social club for the young adult offspring of Springfield's elite. The festive dance introduced 18 year old Susie into Springfield society.[10] After that party, the guest lists published in the newspapers for every social occasion of note from 1880 through 1883 always included Susie Lawrence. For example, she and her parents were among the guests at the wedding of Ella Cullom, daughter of Governor Shelby Cullom.[11]

Even some of her romantic interests were documented in the newspapers. According to news reports, on January 1, 1880, Susie invited Ed Payne to a leap year party at the Leland Hotel.[12] At that time Payne was a young bank teller with a promising future in the financial business. In later life he would be one of Rheuna's partners who established the State National Bank. Rheuna was the bank's first president, and Payne assumed that position at Rheuna's death. Ed Payne, however, was not destined to be a member of Rheuna's family because by December 20, 1882, Edwin Dana, Susie's future husband, was her escort to another dance at the Leland.[13]

Susie's world extended beyond Springfield. The newspapers noted on several occasions that Susie and her mother took trips to Chicago and Lincoln, Illinois, a town 30 miles north of Springfield. She was such a fixture in the social scene that the press chose to note when she was "confined to her bed with sickness."[14] Rheuna and Mary Lawrence's lovely daughter was at the top of the Springfield social ladder. They had provided a life of privilege and entitlement for her. Yet Susie grew up with a father who "abhorred ostentation" and a mother characterized by Frank Lloyd Wright in his *Autobiography* as "dear old Mother Lawrence—salt-risen bread, blackberry preserves."[15] The contradiction between her parent's lifestyle and the social world in which she found herself created an identity ambivalence that plagued Susie for the rest of her life. Susie Lawrence was destined to assume many roles and multiple names as her world constantly changed around her, and she attempted to find her place in those worlds.

Notes for Chapter 1:

1. Susan Lawrence Gehrmann to anonymous, Box 1, Folder 2, Susan L. Dana Bice Collection, Abraham Lincoln Presidential Library & Museum (ALPLM) (hereafter cited as Dana Bice Collection).
2. "Memoranda In Memoriam," Box 1, Folder 4, Dana Bice Collection.
3. "Lincoln colored home is transferred," *Illinois State Register,* May 3, 1906, p. 12.
4. Hendricks, Wanda, *Gender, Race, Politics in the Midwest; Black Club Women in Illinois* (Bloomington, Indiana: University Press,1998), p. 85.
5. *Catalogue of the Bettie Stuart Institute, Springfield, Illinois, 1869-70* (Springfield: John H. Johnson, 1870) and *Catalogue of the Bettie Stuart Institute, Springfield, Illinois,1870-71* (Springfield: Illinois State Register Printing House, 1871) Sangamon Valley Collection, Lincoln Public Library.
6. *History of Sangamon County, Illinois: Together with Sketches of Its Cities*, Inter-state Publishing Co., 1881, pp. 598-9.
7. "An enjoyable concert," *Illinois State Journal,* February 18, 1876, p. 4.
8. "The city," *Illinois State Journal*, December 8, 1876, p. 4.
9. "Art display," *Illinois State Journal*, June 16, 1883, p. 6.
10. "General gossip," *Illinois State Journal,* February 8, 1879, p. 4.
11. "By cupid's art," *Illinois State Journal,* October 25, 1882, p. 6.
12. "New Year's day," *Illinois State Journal,* January 3, 1880, p. 3.
13. "Local notes and personals," *Illinois State Journal,* December 21, 1882, p. 6.
14. "Local notes and personals," *Illinois State Journal*, April 29, 1882, p. 6.
15. Wright, Frank Lloyd, *An Autobiography* (New York: Duell, Sloan and Pearce, 1943), p. 253

2

Susie Dana: Bride and Mother

The house at Fourth and Wright Streets was once again the scene of a joyous celebration. According to a florid newspaper account, Susie Lawrence entered "upon woman's highest sphere in life" when she married Edwin Ward Dillingham Dana on December 4, 1883, in her parent's home.[1] Reverend Peter Wallace of Saybrook, Illinois, not only officiated at the wedding but also baptized the bride as "Susie Lawrence" with no middle name or initial. After the 10 a.m. ceremony, which was witnessed by a few friends and family members, everyone sat down to a celebratory wedding dinner. At noon the young couple was driven to the Chicago & Alton Depot. There they boarded a train to their new home in Minneapolis, Minnesota, where Edwin was engaged in the real estate business.

The journalist who reported the wedding of Susie and Edwin pointed out that the marriage "robs the doting father and mother...of an only child and Springfield society of one of its brightest ornaments." The parents had lost "the dearest object of their earthly affections."[2] However, Susie did not sever her parental or Springfield connections for long. After the December 4, 1883, wedding, she was back in town to assist Mrs. C. M. Smith, a neighbor of her parents, in welcoming guests at the traditional open house on New Year's Day, 1884. Despite the fact that her address was Minneapolis, Susie remained a constant figure on the Springfield newspaper society pages. On New Year's Day 1885, for example, she assisted her mother at her New Year's Day open house,[3] and on February 3 of that year, gowned in wine colored velvet with satin embossed flowers over the front, she attended Governor Oglesby's inaugural reception.[4]

21 Year Old Susie Lawrence
Dana-Thomas House Archives

Susie's new husband, twenty year old Edwin Dana, was born in Burlington, Vermont, in 1863. He grew up in Lincoln, Illinois, where his family moved when he was a toddler. His father, Henry Ward Dana, was a Lincoln attorney who owned the Logan County Abstract Office which also advertised as a real estate, loan and collection agency.[5] Like Rheuna, the senior Dana was a successful entrepreneur. He was involved in multiple enterprises in both Logan County, Illinois, and in Minnesota. The two men were business associates.

Edwin moved to Minneapolis sometime after 1880 to take advantage of the real estate business opportunities in that city. The population of

Ad in Lincoln, Illinois City Directory
Dana-Bice Collection

Minneapolis grew from 47,000 in 1880 to nearly 75,000 by 1883.[6] With the help of his father, Edwin established E. W. Dana & Co., Real Estate and Loans at 319 Nicollet Avenue in Minneapolis.[7] The newlyweds established a home in Minneapolis, and by 1885 the "E. W. Dana & Co. [was] doing a very good business" according to the 1885 issue of *Real Estate and Building Review*.[8]

That same year Edwin and Susie were excited to learn that Susie was pregnant. Although most Victorian women removed themselves from society during their pregnancies, Susie remained very active. She traveled frequently to visit her parents in Springfield. There she continued to lead a busy social life. A pregnant Susie even took classes at what was then called Mrs. Brooks' Art School, and a large panel of hollyhocks painted by her was exhibited at the school's student show that year.[9] The dreams of both Susie and Edwin were fulfilled when Lawrence Henry Dana was born on December 19, 1885. The little boy only lived 12 hours.

Finding emotional support from her parents, Susie continued her travels between the two cities. She spent three weeks in her parent's home in October of the next year. Returning to Minneapolis, she became pregnant again. Following the pattern she had established with her first pregnancy, Susie returned to her parental home for support and again honed her creative skills at Mrs. Brooks' Art School. In June of 1887 a still life study by Susie Dana was displayed at the school's student exhibition.[10] On August 22, 1887, just two months later, Edwin Whitney Dana was born to Susie and Edwin. Little Edwin was not yet 2 months old when he died on October 5. The grieving parents and grandparents buried the baby beside his brother in the family plot in Springfield's Oak Ridge Cemetery.

After two devastating losses, Susie and Edwin were confronted with another catastrophe. The Minneapolis real estate bubble burst in 1890, and the couple's income dropped substantially. No longer able to maintain the life they had come to expect, Edwin changed professions in 1892. He opened the Western Business Agency at 912-916 Guaranty Building in Minneapolis, a company which offered "[to] secure partners and capital for parties wishing to increase their business, [to] locate manufactories of all kinds, and...[to] furnish businessmen generally with high grade clerks...fields of practice found for physicians, lawyers and other professional men." The officers of the company were E.W. Dana, President, J. A. Sims, Secretary, and S. L. Dana, Treasurer.[11] Edwin was a business consultant and head hunter, and Susie, who had no prior business experience, was handling the money for the company. The identity and responsibilities of J. A. Sims are unknown.

Since the entire country experienced an economic panic in 1893, the time was not good for a start-up business. The couple found themselves heavily in debt. A surviving note indicates that H. L. Hach of Hennepin County, Minnesota, sued Susie and Edwin Dana for a promissory note of $500 in 1890. Other records reveal that Susie Dana was sued by Ella Haseltine, John T. West, and the Bank of Minneapolis during that period.[12] In desperation, they sold their Minneapolis home to Susie's mother in February, 1893, for $15,000 less $7,500 in mortgages and briefly established a home on Dearborn Street in Chicago, Illinois.[13] The Western Business Agency relocated to 218 LaSalle Street, Chicago. An ad for the Company boasted branches in Minneapolis, St. Louis, Kansas City, Omaha, Denver, St. Paul, Los Angeles, Buffalo, and West Superior.[14]

Mrs. E. W. Dana, Minneapolis, Minnesota
Dana-Thomas House Archives

The move to Chicago did not improve the couple's situation. Fully aware of Susie's lavish spending habits, Rheuna and Mary continued to indulge their only daughter and came to the couple's rescue. Rheuna paid the taxes on the Minneapolis property the year before Mary bought it.[15] Undoubtedly, Susie's parents settled the other debts. Despite the assistance, the short-lived Western Business Agency failed, and in 1894, a year after moving to Chicago, Susie and Edwin made one more move—back to her Springfield parental home, childless and in debt.

Adversity did not strengthen the relationship of Susie and Edwin but drove Susie closer to her accommodating parents. For example, in 1891 at the depth of their financial crisis, Susie spent several weeks at her parents' home in January, Mary was in Minneapolis for three months in the spring, and in August Mary and Susie took an extended trip to visit relatives in Colorado where Rheuna joined them briefly. Susie returned to Springfield for two funerals in 1892. Her beloved grandmother, Susan Minerva Lawrence, died August 5, and her maternal grandfather, John C. Maxcy, passed away on December 3. Services for both of them were held in the home of Rheuna and Mary.

The newspaper account of their wedding predicted that "the pathway of this worthy young couple [would] be strewn with roses."[16] Unfortunately, the pathway was covered with thorns. After almost 10 years of marriage, Susie and Edwin were back in the fold of her indulgent parents. At 32 years of age, Susie was still primarily a daughter, not a wife or mother.

Notes for Chapter 2

1. "Wedding bells," *Illinois State Register*, December 5, 1883, p. 3.
2. Ibid..
3. "The new year," *Illinois State Journal, January 1, 1885, p. 5.*
4. "Inaugural reception," *Illinois State Journal*, February 4, 1885, p. 8.
5. *City of Lincoln Directory*, 1871-72.
6. Edgar, William C., *The Minneapolis Club: A Review of its History 1883-1920 (*Minneapolis: Minneapolis Club, 1974).
7. *Minneapolis City Directory*, D. R. Davison Co., Minneapolis, 1884 and 1885.
8. "Real Estate Dealers," *Real Estate and Building Review,* Minneapolis, March 19, 1885, p. 2.
9. "Mrs. Brooks' art school," *Illinois State Journal*, June 12, 1885, p. 8.
10. "Art reception," *Illinois State Journal,* June 10, 1887, p. 4.
11. *Minneapolis City Directory*, D.R. Davison Co., Minneapolis, 1892.
12. *Sangamon County Defendant Indexes*, Sangamon County Circuit Clerk's Office, Book 6—1892-1896.
13. "Chicago, Illinois," *City Directories of the United States, 1882-1901,* (Connecticut:Research Publications, 1985).
14. *Chicago City Directory*, 1893.
15. Deed, Box 1 ½, Folder 13, Dana Bice Collection.
16. "Wedding bells," *Illinois State Register,* December 5, 1883, p. 3.

3

Mrs. E. W. Dana: One of the "Four Hundred"

Susie and Edwin ascended from near poverty in Minneapolis and Chicago to membership in the "Four Hundred" of Springfield with ease. The "Four Hundred" was a term coined by Ward McAllister, a self-appointed taste maker in New York City in the mid to late 1800s. McAllister created a list of the people in that city who "really mattered," and the expression "Four Hundred" came to designate the elite in any city. The Springfield "Four Hundred" led the social affairs in the Illinois capital city. Their families controlled the money and wielded the power. They partied, they traveled, and they joined clubs.

The stately home of Rheuna and Mary became the scene of many parties hosted by Susie and Edwin, and, according to newspaper accounts, the couple attended almost every ball, reception, play, card party (euchre and whist), and dinner party that was given in Springfield. They were friends with governors. Susie assisted Mrs. Altgeld, the governor's wife, at a Mansion reception for the Illinois University Glee Club in 1895.[1] Always fashionably dressed, she wore a Nile green brocaded silk dress with iridescent and sable trimmings to Governor Tanner's inaugural ball in January of 1897.[2] Edwin's sister Mabel came by train from her home in Lincoln, Illinois, and joined the golden couple at many of these events. Like other family members and friends from out of town, Mable stayed at Rheuna and Mary's home for extended periods of time.

Easy travel was a relatively new concept in the 1890s. At the beginning of the 19th century, rivers, canals, and horse-drawn coaches were the primary modes of transportation in America. The emergence of the train provided speed and the ability to travel regardless of the weather. With the addition of Pullman's sleeping cars and the new concept of dining cars, those who could afford it moved from one city to another in luxury. When the transcontinental railway was completed in 1869, the entire nation was opened to travelers.

With trains from Springfield traveling daily to the Midwest hub of Chicago, the Lawrence/Dana family took advantage of the convenient and comfortable way to travel the country. Susie and her mother took the train to Chicago repeatedly. In March of 1894 the entire household (Rheuna, Mary, Flora, Susie, and Edwin) traveled to San Francisco,[3] and in February of 1895, Susie, her mother, and Edwin attended the Mardi Gras in New Orleans.[4] Each of these cities was the home of extended family members, and Susie and Mary also often visited other family members in Colorado and Utah.

Susie and her parents joined 54 other Springfield residents on a unique train trip in early July of 1897. They were ostensibly going to the annual conference of the Christian Endeavor in San Francisco which opened July 7, but the Lawrence family had relatives in that area whom they visited frequently. The Christian Endeavor was an organization created in Portland, Maine, in 1881 by Pastor Francis E. Clark to encourage religious fervor and leadership among youth. According to Clark, by 1897 the organization had over 50,000 societies and nearly three million members worldwide. There were 300,000 delegates to the San Francisco conference, and 40,000 of them came by train.[5] The event presented a monumental challenge for the train system. Every Pullman and Tourist car in the country was in service, and the routing of so many trains to one destination from multiple directions was a logistical nightmare for railroad authorities. Many of the passengers in those trains were not Endeavor pilgrims. Individuals from throughout the country took advantage of the low fare to California, and because there were so many stops along the way to avoid other trains, the trip was a long one.

The adventure was high spirited and, in many cases, one big party. The Springfield contingent was no exception. In a nod to the original purpose of the excursion, the three ministers accompanying the Springfield delegation conducted daily devotional services. Susie and Mary provided entertainment. Isaac R. Diller, one of the other "pilgrims" on the train, sent a letter from Carlin, Nevada, to Springfield's *Illinois State Journal* describing the adventures of the Springfield group. According to Diller, Mrs. E. W. Dana, assisted by her mother Mrs. R. D. Lawrence, issued invitations several days in advance for a reception from 3 to 6 on an appointed day. The train was elaborately decorated by the hostesses with pressed flowers "gathered at Tennessee Pass, sweet peas from Salt Lake City, and sage brush." When the guests were assembled, Susie and Mary led them in a game in which guests answered questions from cards prepared by the hostesses. After 20 minutes, Susie and Mary collected the cards, selected the best answers, and awarded prizes. At the next stop, the prize winners jubilantly paraded on the side of the tracks and had their picture taken. Susie and Mary certainly proved Diller's point when he wrote, "The hospitality of the hostesses is too well known to require mention."[6] They could throw a party anytime and anywhere.

Rheuna paid most of the bills generated by this lavish lifestyle. The income from Edwin's fledgling Springfield real estate business, housed in a building owned by Rheuna, could not have supported the expenses that he and Susie incurred. For two and a half years, Edwin fit well into the life provided by his father-in-law in his adopted city. In addition to entertaining and traveling with his wife, he went on extended hunting excursions with friends to Havana and Meredosia, Illinois. In 1897 he was elected one of five directors of the Sangamo Club.[7] At this newly established exclusive organization gentlemen could "take strangers and entertain them in a fitting manner, and where they can meet at will for social conversation and innocent recreation."[8] Rheuna was one of the Club's 120 founders.

Like other women of her era, Susie was a joiner of clubs. She was a member of such organizations as the Every Other Monday Club, Every Wednesday Club, and the South Side Whist Club. Typically activities of those clubs ranged from social events to literary exchanges to charitable efforts. Then in the 1890s, a new concept for woman's clubs emerged nationally. Women all over the country were organizing to create an avenue for self-education and community service. The specific purposes of the clubs varied from city to city. Some actively sought social or moral reform. Others had political agendas such as women's suffrage. Still others, like the Springfield Woman's Club, organized in 1894, promoted self-development. The exploration of knowledge by members of the Springfield club included such topics as "The Value of Art Education in Everyday Life" or "Finance in the Family."[9] Susie was among the charter members of the Springfield club, and like the contrived exclusive "club" of McAllister, the group also boasted 400 members.

Through her affiliation with the Woman's Club, Susie developed for the first time an identity separate from her parents and her husband. She was no longer a daughter or a wife, but a leader among her peers. Susie designed the member pin, chose the organizational colors (pink and green) and flower (rose), and wrote the motto: "There is no Knowledge that is not Power."[10] She served in several leadership positions. As chair of the Art Department, she developed programming in which she, other members, or guests delivered papers on various art related topics which ranged from the aesthetic ("Ancient Art") to the practical ("How to Hang a Picture").[11]

Susie was able to demonstrate her considerable artistic talent to the entire community through her involvement with the Woman's Club. The club was invited to create a woman's page for the January 1, 1896, issue of the *Springfield Evening News*. Susie was the art director for that project.[12] Other than the student art shows, Susie's artistic accomplishments were limited to private projects prior to that time. She had designed a valentine for Edwin in 1891 which she called "An Effect in Blue." It was a multi-page poem illustrated with beautiful drawings. Susie also experimented in photography. Items of photographic equipment were listed in the 1944 auction sale of Susan's possessions, and Frank Lloyd Wright had provided a dark room on the lower level of her home. Her childhood friend, Leigh Gross Day, was an expert photographer who had several books of her work published. Leigh created an album for her daughter Henrietta in which she displayed hand-colored and artistically embellished photographs from Henrietta's early childhood. The enhanced photographs on one page of the album were "taken and finished by Susie L. Dana, May 2, 1900."[13]

A Susie Dana Album

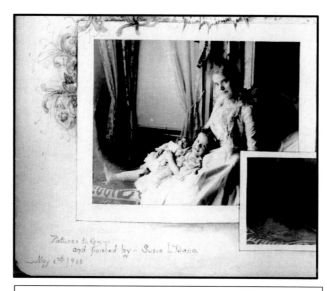

Leigh and Henrietta Day
Photo taken and finished by Susie Dana
"Henrietta Day Album" 1898-1900
Sangamon Valley Collection

Drawings from "An Effect in Blue"
Valentine to Edwin Dana from Susie Dana
Abraham Lincoln Presidential Library & Museum (ALPLM)

The dream of motherhood was still alive for Susie, and she had strong convictions on how children should be raised. She shared her theories on child rearing with other members of the Woman's Club on at least two occasions. One of her presentations was entitled, "Drawing and Color as It Should Be Taught in the Kindergarten." According to a newspaper account of the lecture, "The system that she advocates and has already demonstrated to be practical is highly praised by art critics and teachers in the kindergarten. Her system is entirely original and is so simple that the child is taught the blending of colors unconsciously, and the results are gratifying."[14] At a meeting of the Home and Domestic Department, Susie espoused some very progressive theories on child rearing. Speaking on the topic "Children in the Home," childless Susie "told how often mothers in attempting to show love for their children made slaves of themselves---and tyrants of the little ones. They should be taught self-control and to respect the rights of others---Every child has a right to a happy childhood and the mother must often sacrifice her personal feelings."[15] Doubtless other members of the club questioned her expertise.

Membership in the Springfield Woman's Club also introduced Susie to a new arena: politics. In January of 1897 the State Federation of Woman's Clubs requested that its affiliates support a bill in the Illinois Legislature that was initiated by the State Board of Charities. (Rheuna was a member of that Board.) The bill would "make provision for the children of worthless parents and of the Alms house, etc."[16] The issue was introduced at the club's general meeting, and after much discussion, Susie moved that the club's president "be empowered to cast the vote of the club in favor of the bill for dependent children."[17]

The Springfield Woman's Club added new aspects to Susie's persona, and she thrived. Among other things, she became a public speaker, an advocate for children and the arts, and a leader among other women. All of these experiences gave her a self confidence that would serve her well as she moved beyond Springfield's "Four Hundred" into the new century that was about to begin.

Notes for Chapter 3:

1. "Will receive the glee club," *Illinois State Journal,* March 20, 1895, p. 3.
2. "He led the march," *Illinois State Journal,* January 12, 1897 p. 5.
3. "Personal and general," *Illinois State Journal, March 15, 1894, p. 5.*
4. Ibid., February 20, 1895, p. 5.
5. Clark, Francis E., *World Wide Endeavor, (Philadelphia and Chicago:* Gillespie and Metzgar Publishing, 1895), pp. 549-561.
6. "Bound for Frisco," *Illinois State Journal*, July 12, 1897, p. 6.
7. "Elected new officers," *Illinois State Journal,* April 6, 1897, p. 5.
8. "Two successful clubs," *Illinois State Journal*, June 1, 1890, p. 1.
9. Springfield Woman's club, Minute Book (1895-1897), vol. 2, p. 45.
10. Ibid. pp. 59-61
11. "Art department," *Illinois State Journal*, Nov. 8, 1895, p. 3.
12. Springfield Woman's club, Minute Book (1896-1899) pp. 58-59.
13. *Henrietta Day Album,* 1898-1900, Sangamon Valley Collection.
14. "Art department," *Illinois State Journal,* December 29, 1895, p. 6.
15. Springfield Woman's club, Minute Book (1896-1899) pp. 53-54.
16. Springfield Woman's club, Minute Book (1896-97), vol. 1, p. 51.
17. Ibid.

4

Susie Dana: Widow

Edwin's Springfield real estate business did not prosper, so Rheuna sought another vocation for his son-in-law. By 1897 Rheuna had added gold, silver, and copper mining to his list of business interests. He and other Springfield investors owned the Mahala Mining Company of Leadville, Colorado. In November of that year, Rheuna expanded his mining interests. A "Statement of Incorporation of the Lawrence Mining Co." was filed with the office of the Illinois Secretary of State by Rheuna Lawrence, James A. Connolly, and Thomas Mather. The purpose of the company was "the purchase and sale of gold, silver, and copper mines and mining claims and mining for precious metals in the states of Oregon, Washington, Idaho, Montana, and California." The Secretary of State issued a license listing four investors in the new company: Rheuna Lawrence, James A. Connolly (1,600 shares each), Isaac Brigham (2,400 shares), and E. W. Dana (800 shares).[1] Edwin, who had previously held only white-collar jobs, became a miner.

Earlier in November of 1897, Edwin and "Major" Connolly traveled to Oregon presumably to investigate the mining possibilities in that part of the country. By January of 1898, the *Oregon Observer*, published in Grants Pass, Oregon, was chronicling the progress of E. W. Dana, treasurer of the Lawrence Mining Company, as he began development work in two mines near Leland, Oregon—the Lawrence and the Copper Stain.[2] The Copper Stain Mine showed promise, and Edwin and "his associates" (Rheuna and other partners) purchased the property. Edwin continued overseeing the development of the mine, reporting to the newspaper that "the property is showing up splendidly. They are down 160 feet and keep 12 men at work running day and night."[3] In a letter to Rheuna on August 29, 1900, Edwin wrote, "I have quit work over at the Lawrence for the present." He continued to outline his plans for roads around the Copper Stain, to discuss financial support for the project, and to seek approval of his business decisions from his father-in-law.[4]

Susie and Edwin began a commuter marriage. For the most part, Susie remained in Springfield, but the custom of the day was that women of means would escape the heat of Springfield summers and the cold of the winters by traveling to other parts of the country. Susie frequently visited her husband in Oregon particularly in the summers. The accommodations at the mine were primitive as evidenced by a letter to Susie from Edwin: "It's real hot, have been fighting bed bugs yesterday afternoon, last night, and this morning. I believe the cabin is alive with them. They must drop out of the ceiling on to the head as I have the legs of the bed in water. Still they got on."[5] Consequently, during her visits Susie generally stayed about 16 miles from the mine in a hotel in Grants Pass, the closest large town.

Often accompanied by her mother, Susie continued the practice of visiting friends and relatives in various other cities such as New Orleans, Chicago, and Salt Lake City while Edwin was in Oregon.

The miles between Oregon and Illinois generated frequent correspondence, and a bundle of letters survives from that period with a note in Susie's handwriting which reads: "Personal letters E.W. Dana to Susan Lawrence Dana, Rheuna D. Lawrence to Susan Lawrence Dana. Kept for a matter of sentiment—destroy when I am dead—of no value to anyone but me. Susan Lawrence Dana"[6] Fortunately the letters were not destroyed because they present a brief story of the Oregon mine venture and an insight into the family dynamics.

Rheuna expressed frustration in August, 1899, letters to Susie who, with her mother, was visiting Edwin in Oregon:

> August 5: I can't work myself up to think there will be any mining to pay Ed to remain there…Leadville [Colorado] is no good. No ore of pay value and a bad smelter strike on.
>
> August 11: I am not very lucky in Oregon.
>
> August 31: I wish Ed could make a good strike out there.[7]

Edwin's letters to Rheuna, which he addressed "My dear Father," reveals a warm respect for his in-laws as well as a sense of humor. Edwin writes: "Suppose you will get one of those horseless carriages. If you do, tell Mama not to jerk on the lines. It won't do any good." His letters to Susan were affectionate and solicitous. He signed his July 10, 1900, letter: "Hope you can keep cool. Don't go out much in the sun—with dearest love and kisses I am as ever yours, Ed."[8] He sought special gifts for his wife for he wrote: "The first time I am in town I will try and match the nugget for you given I can find one somewhere that will do."[9]

Although Susie was a married woman in her mid-thirties, Rheuna addressed all of his letters to her with "Dear Tag," her childhood nick-name. He signed them "Your old Papa" or "Dadie as Ever." The major subject of his letters was the weather. He included many details of domestic life in their Springfield home and local gossip but very little information about his business, political, or public service life despite the fact that he was serving on the Illinois Board of Public Charities, president of the State National Bank, and president of Springfield's Board of Education at the time. In one letter Rheuna, always the doting father, assured Susie that he paid all of the bills that she and her mother had accumulated.

Excerpt of Rheuna Letter
Dana Bice Collection

Only two letters from Susie to Edwin survive from the time he was in Oregon. In both letters she describes her extreme physical discomfort:

August 29, 1900: The change to cooler weather has kept my lung paining me a great deal and last night I awakened several times finding it almost impossible to turn over. The suffering was dreadful. I began taking something for my kidneys today. Hope they will improve.
September 1, 1900: I have felt so miserable. I have been no comfort to myself...I went to bed last night at seven and did not sleep until after three this morning.[10]

Susie was plagued by multiple ailments most of her life. She once wrote, "I have so many times [had] severe illness. Three times I have been given up to die."[11] Rheuna was called to the Minneapolis bedside of Susie who was "seriously ill"[12] just three months after her wedding. Fifteen years later Edwin rushed to Springfield from Oregon "on receiving news of the serious illness of his wife."[13] Each time she seemed to recover and continue an active life.

The Oregon chapter in Susie's life ended abruptly on one devastating weekend in September, 1900. Susie was planning to meet Edwin in Grants Pass on Saturday, September 1. Then she received a note from him in which he regretfully explained that he would not be able to join her until Monday night or Tuesday. She sent a note back to him on the Saturday evening train expressing her disappointment.[14] He never received the note. On Monday, September 3, C. D. Burnett, a miner who worked with Edwin at the Copper Stain Mine, arrived at the hotel where she was waiting for Edwin to deliver life changing news to Susie. Burnett had traveled the 16 mile horse trail from the mine to Grants Pass to tell her that Edwin had been killed Sunday in a terrible mining accident. The harness on the horses that were powering a hoisting machine broke causing the lever to spring back. The lever hit Edwin with full force across the chest. He died instantly.[15]

Susie immediately telegraphed her father. With the assistance of C. D. Burnett and Edwin Dana's brother Will who also worked at the mine, the grief stricken widow made arrangements to have the body embalmed in Grants Pass.[16] By Tuesday night Will and Susie were on a train with Edwin's body en route to Minneapolis. When he received the telegram, Rheuna immediately made train reservations to meet them in Minneapolis and to accompany them back to Springfield. There, after a funeral service in the Lawrence home, 36 year old Edwin Dana was buried in the Lawrence family plot in Oak Ridge Cemetery beside his two infant sons.

The ideal roles for women of Susie's era were wife and mother. Both had been tragically snatched from Susie by death. After almost 17 years of marriage, 37 year old Susie Lawrence assumed her new role in society— that of a widow.

Notes for Chapter 4:

1. Incorporation Papers, Illinois Secretary of State's Records, November 27, 1897.
2. "Mining news," *Oregon Observer*, January 22, 1898, p. 7.
3. "Personal," *Oregon Observer*, April 21, 1900, p. 5.
4. Edwin Dana to Rheuna Lawrence, August 29, 1900, Box 1 1/2, Folder 2, Dana Bice Collection.
5. Edwin Dana to Susan Dana, July 10, 1900, Box 1 1/2, Folder 2, Dana Bice Collection.
6. Susan Dana note, undated, Box 1 1/2, Folder 2, Dana Bice Collection.
7. Rheuna Lawrence to Susan Dana, August 5 to 31, 1899, Box 1 1/2, Folder 2, Dana Bice Collection.
8. Edwin Dana to Susan Dana, July 10, 1900, Box 1 1/2, Folder 2, Dana Bice Collection.
9. Edwin Dana to Susan Dana, March 18, 1900, Box 1 1/2, Folder 2, Dana Bice Collection.
10. Susan Dana to Edwin Dana, August 29 and September 1, 1900, Box 1 1/2, Folder 2, Dana Bice Collection.
11. Susan Dana to anonymous, Box 1, Folder 15, Dana Bice Collection.
12. "Local breveties," *Illinois State Journal*, March 13, 1884, p. 8.
13. "Personal," *Oregon Observer*, May 13, 1899, p. 7.
14. Susan Dana to Edwin Dana, September 1, 1900, Box 1 1/2, Folder 2, Dana Bice Collection.
15. "Death of Edwin Dana," *Illinois State Journal*, September 4, 1900.
16. "E. W. Dana's sudden death," *Oregon Observer*, September 8, 1900.

5

Susie Lawrence Dana: Heiress

There was very little celebrating at the Lawrence home on South Fourth Street on New Year's Day, 1901. The family was still mourning Edwin who had died just three months earlier, and Rheuna was seriously ill. When he made the heart-breaking trip to meet Susie in Minneapolis, he was beginning to feel symptoms of what would later be diagnosed as liver disease. His condition deteriorated, and by mid-January he could no longer leave his room. Sixty-four year old Rheuna finally succumbed to what was diagnosed as liver atrophy with complications on Sunday afternoon, February 17, 1901. Susie and Mary were at his bedside.

On Wednesday of that week the home was once again the scene of a funeral service. The Knights Templar were in charge, and Masonic rites were conducted at the graveside in Oak Ridge Cemetery. The many mourners included state and local officials, business associates, friends, and neighbors. Springfield had lost one of its most prominent citizens, and the Lawrence women no longer had their anchor.

Suddenly Susie was thrust into an unexpected role. In six months she had lost the two men who took care of her. Her mother was grief-stricken. There was no one else to make decisions or to assume responsibilities. Susie quickly adapted to the drastic changes in her life.

The first indication of Susie's new-found ability to assume control of her own destiny emerged when Rheuna's will was filed for probate in Sangamon County Court on March 19, a month after he died. Mary and Susie were listed as primary beneficiaries. Other heirs included Flora C. Lawrence, Marie Georgia (Lawrence) Jefferson, Marie D. Lawrence, William J. Downs and wife, Jessie R. Hudgins, William L. Robbins, Agnes M. Zane (all relatives) and E.W. Dana (deceased son-in-law)[1] However, in April County Judge G. W. Murray ruled that the will was not entitled to probate or record because the witnesses (Herman Pierik and Joseph F. Bunn, officers in the State National Bank) testified that Rheuna did not sign the will in their presence. The will was turned over to Susie, and she was directed to preserve it. It was never seen again. Furthermore, in an unprecedented move, Judge Murray gave Susie permission to withdraw the will from the county record. Through this maneuver, no one else could access the contents of the will, and Susie obtained sole control of Rheuna's holdings.

At her mother's request, Susie was officially named administrator of the estate. She paid the relatives the sum of money specified in the disqualified will. The amount of the remaining estate is unclear. On April 14, 1901, Susie filed an inventory of Rheuna's estate with Sangamon County. The inventory vaguely listed real estate of "unknown" value and $66,725.00 worth of notes, stocks, bonds,

and cash.[2] Since Rheuna owned lead and gold mines in both Colorado and Oregon as well as property throughout Sangamon and Logan Counties, the real estate holdings were undoubtedly worth a very large sum. While it is impossible to state the exact amount of Susie's inheritance, years later the writer of her obituary estimated that Rheuna's estate was valued at $3,000,000.[3]

Susie promptly took an active interest in her newly acquired business ventures. She, her mother, and Cousin Florence traveled to Grants Pass, Oregon, in late June of 1901, and Susie frequently visited the Copper Stain Mine that summer. Although the three women returned to Springfield in late August, Susie again traveled to Grants Pass in October.[4] Edwin's brother Will Dana, then superintendent of the mine, undoubtedly had ambivalent reactions when his sister-in-law with no knowledge of the mining industry came to "supervise" the operation. Since there is no evidence of any other visits by Susie, it can be assumed that she chose to be an absentee owner after her initial burst of interest.

The ties between daughter and father were not broken by death. Susie was fixated on keeping Rheuna's memory alive. After his death, she took measurements of his head "for use in case they should be wanted to make a bust of him."[5] In a lavish gesture typical of Susie, she had a mourning brooch with a cameo of her father's head surrounded by 35 matching diamonds created to honor him.[6]

Susie chose to memorialize her father in a public way through the Springfield school system. Rheuna had been a member of the Board of Education from 1893 to his death in 1901. He served as president the last six years of his life. In July of 1902 Susie proposed to the Board that two annual student contests be established with "Rheuna D. Lawrence Memorial Prizes" going to the winners. She and her mother underwrote the project. One competition would be a high school oratorical contest, and the other would be for manual training students "who by close application and persistent effort shall attain the highest skill and proficiency in this department." The latter was to honor her father's interest in "industrial education and the high esteem he placed on all honest manual labor." The Board approved her proposal.[7] The first oratorical contest was held in April, 1903, with 20 gold dollars for the first prize and 10 dollars for the second prize. The manual training first prize winner received 10 dollars, and the second place winner went home with five dollars in June of that year.[8]

Lawrence Library
Dana-Thomas House Archives

Meanwhile, at their February, 1903, meeting the School Board voted to name the new elementary school that was being built on Springfield's sparsely populated south side the "Lawrence School" in honor of Rheuna.[9] Susie commissioned Frank Lloyd Wright, the young architect who was remodeling her father's home at the time, to design a library for the new school. She also funded the library's Wright-designed furniture, and she purchased books for the library. In the words of a local reporter, the results were "the most beautiful and artistic school library in the city."[10] Susie had created a lasting memorial to Rheuna from his "Tag."

Bookplate
Dana Bice Collection

23

Notes for Chapter 5:

1. Legal notice, *Illinois State Journal*, March 20, 1901.
2. Inventory Record No. 19, Sangamon County, Illinois, 1900-1902, Rheuna D. Lawrence, IRAD collection, University of Illinois Springfield.
3. "Mrs. Susan Lawrence dies at St. John's hospital," *Illinois State Journal,* February 21, 1946.
4. *Oregon Observer*, July 2, 19001, August 7, 1901, and August 31, 1901.
5. Susan Lawrence Dana note, Box 1, Folder 12, Dana/Bice Collection.
6. Appraisal Inventory, Susan Z. Lawrence, Incompetency File #5908, Sangamon County Circuit Clerk's Office, Springfield.
7. Springfield Board of Education Minutes, August 5, 1902, Sangamon Valley Collection, Lincoln Public Library, Springfield, Illinois (hereafter cited as SVC).
8. "Will contest for prizes," *Illinois State Journal*, May 24, 1903.
9. Springfield Board of Education Minutes, February 3, 1903, SVC.
10. "The social side," *Illinois State Register*, April 14, 1906.

6

Susan Lawrence Dana: Home Builder and Traveler

Sometime in 1901 or 1902 Susan met Frank Lloyd Wright, an emerging young architect from Oak Park, Illinois. His body of work at that time included 60 houses in the Chicago area and two in Kankakee, Illinois, all of which were controversial for their unique designs. Wright was promoting his unconventional architectural philosophy widely through Chicago exhibits, lectures, and publications. The design of one of the Kankakee homes was in an article entitled "A Home in a Prairie Town" published in the February, 1901, issue of *Ladies' Home Journal.*[1] His unconventional approach to creating living spaces appealed to Susan, and in a move to establish her individual identity, she commissioned him to remodel her father's house.

The project began in the summer of 1902 with new walls erected around the original building. The local press briefly noticed the activity:

> Excavation has been completed at the Lawrence home and work of remodeling the home of the widow of the former president of the Springfield board of education soon will be well under way. An entirely new roof of tile will be one of the many improvements.[2]

New/Old House
Dana-Thomas Archives

Wright's original drawings for the house did indeed focus on retaining much of the old house. However, revised drawings dated January 18, 1903, expanded the original plans, rearranged spaces, and retained only a few walls of the original building. In homage to Rheuna, the fireplace from his

Italianate home was preserved in a small sitting room that could be closed off from the rest of the house.

To accommodate the expanded plans, the eight-room cottage that Rheuna had built on the southwest corner of the property was moved across Third Street and placed on a new foundation on that lot. Susan, her mother, and Cousin Flora lived in that house during the construction. Since no correspondence or financial records have survived, the price of the project is unknown. Reportedly Susan gave Wright an open check book, and cost estimates range from $65,000 to $125,000 for the building, furniture, light fixtures, and leaded art glass.

Walls of New House
Dana-Thomas House Archives

An anomaly in Springfield, the completed house was a masterpiece that still stands today as one of Wright's finest Prairie designs. With an open floor plan, the blonde Roman brick home has 35 rooms on 16 different levels. The rooms include three two-story social spaces: the reception area, the dining room, and the gallery with a small stage. Each of these is overlooked by a musician's balcony. Wright designed more than 100 pieces of furniture, 250 leaded art glass windows and doors, and over 100 art glass fixtures for the 12,600 square feet of space. He unified the complex art glass with the repeated motifs of the butterfly and the sumac plant. In addition to providing accommodations for Susan to display her art and pottery collection, Wright incorporated three original works of art into the design. "Flower in a Crannied Wall," a terracotta sculpture by Richard Bock, greeted visitors in the vestibule, and another, "Moon Children," was constructed in the reception hall. A mural by George Niedecken surrounded guests in the dining room. Additionally, Wright included a library, duck pin alley, and private suites for Susan, Mary, Cousin Florence, and the live-in help. Each of the four sleeping areas had a full bath. The remodeled carriage house, garden, and house were all enclosed by a dramatic wall made of bricks that matched the house.

A Wright Designed Glass Gallery

The Lawrence House

In Mary's Bathroom

Sumac in Dining Room

Torii Window in Gallery

In Susan's Bedroom

All images from Dana-Thomas House Archives

Frank Lloyd Wright only visited Springfield occasionally during the building process. The supervising architect was Samuel Jackson (S. J.) Hanes, a local architect whose office was on the third floor of the Lincoln/Herndon Building in downtown Springfield. Since Susan and Hanes moved in the same social circles, she may have introduced him to Wright. Another possibility is that Wright knew Hanes through professional contacts. A frequent visitor to Chicago, Hanes was very active in state professional activities. According to his son, Murray Hanes, S. J. was a friend of Louis Sullivan and helped establish the state architectural examination in 1899. The younger Hanes later recalled that Wright would come from Chicago on the train in the morning and return that same day after visiting the site and conferring with S. J. It was the responsibility of S. J. Hanes to supervise the local craftsmen and contractors.[3]

Three women living together in the relatively cramped quarters of the cottage during construction of the new house proved to be difficult. Trusting Hanes to complete the project competently, Susan and Mary escaped through the travel opportunities that their membership in the Daughters of the American Revolution (DAR) offered. Membership in the DAR was limited to women who could trace their lineage to an ancestor who aided in achieving American independence, and Susan claimed two forefathers who contributed to the cause on her application. One was Joel Maxey, a relative of her mother who was buried in Old Salem Cemetery near Springfield, and the other was Uriah Lawrence, an ancestor of her father.[4]

Like the Springfield Woman's Club, the Springfield DAR chapter was organized in 1894. The national DAR had been founded just four years previously in Washington, D.C. Frustrated by their exclusion from men's patriotic organizations, the founding women formed their own association with three objectives: historical, educational, and patriotic. The Springfield chapter was also a philanthropic organization which supported the juvenile court fund and delinquent children expenses.

Through her affiliation with the DAR, Susan developed two new passions: genealogy and expanded travel. Her interest in discovering her family lineage led her to arrange the removal of the remains of Lewis Whitney Lawrence, her paternal grandfather and Rufus Whitney Lawrence, her father's brother, from their burial site in Springfield, Ohio, to the Lawrence family plot in Oak Ridge cemetery in Springfield, Illinois, in 1904.[5] In doing so, she gave one more gift to her father. She reunited him with his family forever.

Active membership in the DAR fostered an expanded world view for Susan. Susan and Mary were named alternate delegates to state and national conferences, and through their travels they met and socialized with women from all over the country. Their first experience at a DAR National Congress was in 1903 when they went to Washington D.C. There they were welcomed at a reception for delegates in the White House by none other than President and Mrs. Theodore Roosevelt. Mother and daughter returned again to the National Congress in Washington the next year, and in October of 1904 the DAR celebrated Founders' Day at the Louisiana Purchase Exposition in St. Louis. A large delegation from Springfield including Susan and Mary enjoyed socializing at the many DAR receptions and the entertainment opportunities that the exposition offered.[6]

At some time during one of the visits to Washington, Susan saw President Roosevelt riding in an elegant carriage designed just for him. When she returned home, she ordered a replica of the presidential carriage for herself. The carriage was delivered to Susan months later, but it was never driven in Springfield. It remained parked until it was sold at auction at the end of Susan's life. Her extravagant tastes had not diminished, and now she could afford anything she wanted—including an elaborate mansion for herself on the property where her father had once proudly built a stately home for his family.

Notes for Chapter 6:

1. Thomson, Lain, *Frank Lloyd Wright, A Visual Encyclopedia* (London:PRC Publishing Limited, 2004), p. 20.
2. "New homes are building," *Illinois State Journal*, September 4, 1902.
3. Murray Hanes, interview by Donald Hallmark, 1982, transcript Dana-Thomas House Collection.
4. DAR application, Illinois Historic Preservation Agency files (hereafter cited as IHPA files).
5. Notes in Susan Lawrence's Hand, Box 1, folder 3, Dana Bice Collection.
6. "Socially speaking," *Springfield News,* October 17, 1904, p. 3.

7

Susan Lawrence Dana (Aunty Dana): Hostess

For Susan the new house which she insisted on calling the Lawrence House was more than a home. It was a center for entertaining, a showcase for the visual and performing arts, and a setting for her developing lifestyle. A glimpse into Susan's new world can be found in this description of the first recorded social event in the new house in October, 1904:

> Mrs. Susan Lawrence Dana of South Fourth street has been entertaining a house party at her home several days, among the guests being Dr. Paul Cohn of Vienna, Austria, editor of the Vienna *Die Zeit*, and vice chairman of the jury of awards, group 13 of the Fine Arts building at the St. Louis fair, Dr. H.A. Cuppy of New York, editor of *Public Opinion*, the well-known magazine and head of the Puritan Pure Food and Chocolate company, Miss Katherine Montgomery, of Madison, Mississippi, Miss Achaah Holloway of Springfield, Ohio, Mrs. George Davis and Miss Farneta Davis of Oakland, California [cousins].[1]

Dramatic shifts in Susan's life can be noted in this announcement. First, only Susan was the hostess. She was not co-hosting with her mother. Second, the global nature of the guest list reveals the extensive contacts she was making beyond Springfield. Seemingly an unconventional cosmopolitan and self-reliant woman was emerging from the sorrows of death and the expectations of her society.

Nine days of gala events introduced the Lawrence House to the Springfield community at the end of December, 1904. The centerpiece of all the parties was the towering Christmas tree with 150 incandescent lights in the gallery. On the tree were ". . . all sorts of toys, dolls, Noah's arks, jumping jacks, woolly dogs, bags and bags of candy, tinsel, icicles, glass balls of all colors; the list is inexhaustible, for every twig seem[ed] to be laden with something."[2]

Susan and Mary opened the celebration on December 20 and 21 with a two-day bazaar for the benefit of the King's Daughters Home. For those two days, booths with games surrounded the tree in the gallery, tables with homemade handiwork and candies for sale stood in the library below, and a country store selling "live chickens, bales of hay and oats, bottles of pickles, olives, coffee pots, bags, brooms, fruit, canned goods, etc."[3] was in the basement. Guests enjoyed refreshments in two Japanese tea rooms adjacent to the country store.

The lavish bazaar that benefited the King's Daughters Home by $334[4] was particularly appropriate because both Susan and her mother were very active in that organization. Mary Lawrence

had been on the executive board which oversaw the purchase and establishment of the home on North Sixth Street in 1895. With funds earned through bazaars, performances, and donations, the organization completely renovated an existing building with all the modern conveniences available to accommodate 20 women over 60 in their declining years. The refurbished home was furnished by individuals and circles of women from churches in Sangamon County. Mary Lawrence equipped the kitchen with her own funds and donations from local hardware merchants.[5] By 1904, continual support for the upkeep of the home was the primary purpose of the circles of the King's Daughters. Susan had decorated booths at bazaars and appeared in dramatic performances to benefit the home in previous years. She had been serving on the board, and her mother had been First Vice President since 1902. After Mary's death, a circle was named in her memory, and each February Susan or Florence entertained the Mary A. Lawrence Circle in the Lawrence House in remembrance of the anniversary of Mary's birth.

The largest and most shocking of the housewarming parties was held on December 23 when Susan and her mother entertained the more than 150 men who built the house and their families. Like the Lawrence House itself, the guest list was a major deviation. Springfield had never witnessed an event where workmen and their families attended a party on Aristocracy Hill. Susan explained her motivation to a reporter:

> "We wanted the children present," said Mrs. Dana, "because we wanted them to see what their fathers had done and thus encourage them to work of the same character. It would not have been possible for careless, or incompetent or indifferent artisans to have brought about the results attained in this building and we felt that it would be gratifying to the

workmen to have the members of their families inspect the work and to know how much we appreciate it."[6]

Workmen's Invitation
Dana Bice Collection

Frank Lloyd Wright with his first wife Catherine and son John traveled from Oak Park, Illinois, for the party. John would later recall that Susan wore Chanel perfume and that she gave a diamond necklace to his mother. Catherine insisted that her husband return it. John also remembered that one of the hod carriers brought his 12 children.[7]

Another guest, painter Fred Hoffman, came without his family. Because his wife Clara was expecting their first child at any time, she asked her husband to express her regrets to the hostess. Susan understood and asked that the couple name the child after her if it was a girl. Then Susan packed a basket of treats including a papier-mâché doll that was hanging on the tree and sent her coachman to Clara with the gifts. On December 28 the baby girl was born, and her parents named her Susan Lawrence Hoffman. The elder Susan assumed the role of honorary godmother. When the young Susan was baptized, "Aunty Dana" gave her a white teddy bear with a bank book hanging from its neck. A bank deposit of $100 was recorded in the book. This was the first of many gifts "Aunty Dana" would give to young Susan. Until she was 18 years old, she received a gift every holiday season, many of which were from European countries where "Aunty Dana" was visiting.

The final party of the "grand opening" of the Lawrence House was a lavish reception on December 29 hosted by the members of the Woman's Club who were celebrating their 10th anniversary. In between the opening benefit for the King's Daughters and the Woman's Club reception, Susan and her mother hosted parties for many of Springfield's most needy citizens. They entertained the residents of the King's Daughter Home for Aged Women, the St. Joseph's Old Folks Home, the

Home for the Friendless, the Orphanage of the Holy Child, and the children of the Dominican Convent. All guest received a souvenir of the occasion.[8]

By extending her generosity to the beneficiaries of charity and the families of workmen to social events in her new home, Susan Lawrence Dana chose to honor her mother's philanthropic spirit and her father's work ethic. At the same time she was reinventing herself as a brand new creature with her own style which matched her environment--the home Frank Lloyd Wright had designed for her. She emerged unconventional, democratic, and dramatic.

Notes for Chapter 7:

1. "Socially speaking," *Springfield News,* October 3, 1904, p. 3.
2. Ibid., December 20, 1904, p. 3.
3. Ibid.
4. Ibid. December 24, 1904, p. 3.
5. "Home for the aged," *Illinois State Journal,* September 16, 1895, p.3.
6. Ibid, December 24, 1904, p. 5.
7. Wright, John Lloyd, *My Father Who Is On Earth* (Carbondale and Edwardsville, Illinois: Southern Illinois University Press, 1994), p. 41.
8. "Socially speaking," *Springfield News*, December 27, 1904, p. 3.

8

Susan Lawrence Dana: Spiritualist

On January 24, 1905, just a month after the festive opening of the Lawrence House, Susan and her mother attended a charity ball at the State Armory sponsored by the Sangamo Club.[1] Two days later they left Springfield for New York to embark on a cruise to the Caribbean. After stops in Cuba and Nassau, the two women began a tour of the southern United States. They visited Palm Beach and Jacksonville, Florida. There they boarded a train on March 12 to Thomasville, Georgia, where they planned to stop for a few days. While en route, Mary became ill. She had been suffering from asthma and "fatty degeneration of the heart," but the trip seemed to have improved her health. Her condition degenerated quickly on the train. Despite the fact that there was a doctor on board who tried to help, she died of cardial asthma within 20 minutes after she was stricken. She was 64 years old. Arrangements were made to remove the body from the train at Way Cross, Georgia, where she was prepared for burial. Suddenly Susan was alone, and once again she accompanied a dead loved one on a train trip home to Springfield.[2]

On March 16, 1905, the Lawrence House became the scene of the first of many funerals that would be conducted there. Pastors of First Methodist Church, Dr. W.N. McElroy and Reverend N.G. Lyons, presided. A newspaper reported that the mourners "came from many walks of life and showed that Mrs. Lawrence in her dealings and charity drew no class or color line distinction, the gathering at the funeral being a lesson in the equality of man." Residents of the Colored Old Folks' and Orphans' Home and the King's Daughters Home for Aged Women knelt at the casket beside members of the Springfield Woman's Club and the Woman's Christian Temperance Union.[3] Mary Agnes Lawrence was buried with her husband and other daughter in Oak Ridge Cemetery.

When confronted with death, Susan did not turn to the faith of her parents. After Edwin's death she wrote to a friend, "My views of life and death are different from those of many." At that time in her life, she firmly believed that ties with the deceased were not severed at death, and she could communicate with them through spiritualism. She was not alone. The supernatural permeated America at the end of the 19th and beginning of the 20th centuries, and women at the top of the social and economic ladders were the most active participants. At its peak at the turn of the century, spiritualism had over 10 million followers. The National Spiritualist Association of America (NSAA) defines spiritualism as "the science, philosophy and religion of continuous life, based upon the demonstrated fact of communication, by means of mediumship, with those who live in the Spirit World." The mediums intervene in a variety of ways either through verbal or physical manifestations.[4]

While Susan was outwardly in control of her new-found independent life, inwardly she was full of self-doubt. Her insecurities were revealed in a set of surviving spirit letters she began exchanging with her deceased husband and father in August, 1904, while the Lawrence House was still under construction. Popular at the turn of the century, spirit writing was a means to communicate with the dead. Proponents of the phenomenon explain that a psychic force passes through a medium and writes messages from the dead to the living.

One of the most famous practitioners of spirit writing was Laura Carter Pruden of Cincinnati, Ohio. Specifically, her method was slate writing. The medium would place a small piece of slate pencil between two large slates, often wrapping them in a cloth. She would then place the slates on the floor and put her foot on them. Soon, scratching from the slates could be heard and then raps to indicate that the message was complete. When they were unwrapped, the slates were purportedly covered with writing.[5] Mrs. Pruden reluctantly performed at least two writings for Susan from a distance. One letter from the medium to Susan read:

> I could not help the delay in sitting for you, for my time has been so engaged, and as it takes so much longer to sit for anyone at a distance. This morning was the very first opportunity I had. I hope the results however will make up for your long waiting. I copied the letter word for word as it appeared on the slate. I would much prefer the presence of the sitter.[6]

Susan may have obtained other letters in person from Mrs. Pruden, or she consulted other spirit writing mediums. The letters that Susan wrote to her deceased family uncover Susan's deepest anxieties regarding her future, men, money, and business.

She asked her dead father, "Shall I enter public life? If so, how soon and on what subject will I lecture?" In another letter she queried, "Shall I sit for slate writing mediumship?" Her aspirations were lofty. "I crave knowledge, wisdom, and money. Surely God will grant them to me when I only want them for the good I can do humanity with them." In her early forties and outwardly successful, she was still seeking her place in the world: "Is there any special preparation I can make towards getting ready for the great life work that God is going to give me to do? Will it be in the lecture field? Will I have any trouble recognizing it when it comes to me to do?"[7]

Spirit Letter Excerpt from Susan to Rheuna
Dana Bice Collection

The need for a man to provide money for her was still ingrained in her: "Will I have to marry Mr. Bradley to get his money or will he leave it to me anyway?" "How will Mr. Bradley die?" "Will Mr. Livingston of New York leave me money?"[8] She sought her father's business advice beyond the grave:

> "Will you tell me what is best to do with the Copper Stain?" "Will we find anything at the Lawrence Mine?" "Can I trust Will Dana to be doing the work there that you want done?" "Shall I try to buy out Clint Burnett's interest in the Copper Stain?" "Shall I pump the water out?" "Shall I invest in Elmer Gates' patent for his casting welders and hygienic light illuminator?"[9]

Rheuna's spirit letter responses were supportive:

> I would be averse to your marrying Mr. Bradley for you could not be happy with him. The present prospects are that he will leave you money anyway. . .Rest assured dear that Ed and I are combining our power and influence toward your best good, and Tag be assured that your heart's desire to acquire knowledge, wisdom and money will be grandly realized in the not distant future. . . We are not at all impressed with Elmer Gates' project. . . The Copper Stain Mine is all right and you will do well to buy C. B.'s interest.[10]

After her mother died, Susan exchanged letters with Mary as well as with Rheuna and Edwin through May of 1905. She sought comfort, guidance, protection, and especially approval from her parents. She asked her father, "Papa, do you know all about the new home, and are you pleased with it? Were you with us at our Christmas tree? Did all of it meet with your approval?" To her mother she inquired, "Shall I go west this year? Shall I take Flora? Do you approve of my not wearing mourning?" All of these queries met with very positive responses. Her mother replied in one letter, "You will not be allowed to make a mistake."[11] These reassurances undoubtedly bolstered Susan's self-confidence.

The Lawrence House became the scene of other spiritualist activities in 1905. Susan referred several times in her letters to a Sunday morning service at her home. These services may have been led by Mary Pickens, a close friend of Susan, who was one of several Springfield mediums. She was also encouraged in the letters by the spirit of her mother to sit by herself in her mother's old room three times a week for help in her "spiritual development," presumably in preparation for her slate writing career. When Mary was living, she did not believe in or approve of the spirit letter phenomena.[12] This seemingly change of attitude must have assured Susan that she was doing the right thing.

Susan's strong will and resiliency came from an inner strength that was fueled by the encouragement she received from the spirit world. Her unorthodox approach to life after death paralleled her unconventional choices in this life.

Notes for Chapter 8:

1. "Success crowns charity ball," *Illinois State Register,* January 25, 1905, p. 3.
2. "News caused profound impression," *Illinois State Register*, March 14, 1905, p. 2.
3. Ibid.
4. Lindgren, Carl Edwin, *Spiritualism: Innocent Beliefs to Scientific Curiosity, 1700s-1800s,*
   http://users.panola.com/lindgren/spirit-1.html
5. Jefts, Lena Barnes, "Telekinesis and Spirit Writing," *Psychic Soul,*
   http://www.psychicsoul.org/print.php?id=164&catid=5
6. Spirit Letters, Box 1, Folder 15, Dana Bice Collection.
7. Ibid.
8. Ibid.
9. Ibid.
10. Ibid.
11. Ibid.
12. Ibid.

9

Susan Lawrence Dana: Butterfly

Despite the fact that Susan internally harbored severe self-doubts, she developed an image in the Springfield community that was legendary. The opening of the Lawrence House launched a seven-year period in which she was a generous philanthropist, a willing volunteer, a flamboyant hostess, and an extensive world traveler. The local newspapers documented most of her extravagant public life.

Susan helped finance many community endeavors during those seven years. She was listed as a patroness of charitable events for such diverse causes as the Humane Society (then dedicated to the prevention of cruelty to children and animals)[1] and the YMCA building.[2] However, her primary interest was support of the arts. She was a patroness for local productions such as an original musical entitled "Sangamon County Fair"[3] and an organ recital at First Methodist Church.[4] Beginning in 1911 Susan helped bring out-of-town performers to Springfield. Not only did she support the University of Illinois Glee Club concert,[5] but she also contributed to the Minneapolis Symphony Orchestra[6] and the Chicago Grand Opera Company[7] performances in Springfield

In addition to her financial donations, Susan contributed her time to many community causes. She served on the Humane Society Board[8] and represented the Mary A. Lawrence Circle on the King's Daughters Board.[9] When the Amateur Art Study Club was formed, Susan became a charter member.[10] The Western Drawing and Manual Training Association met in Springfield for their annual meeting in May of 1911, and Susan volunteered on the display committee.[11] She continued her membership in the Ladies' Soldier's Aid Society[12] and the Woman's Club. Her affiliation with the latter probably influenced the choice by that organization of Frank Lloyd Wright as a lecturer on April 25, 1906. His topic was landscape gardening, and according to a newspaper report, he uncharacteristically declared "that a greater necessity existed for the landscape architect than for the building architect." Despite the fact that the Springfield Men's Association was also invited to the lecture, Wright only attracted a small audience.[13]

Susan's largest volunteer commitment was to the DAR during that period of her life. The organization sponsored an elaborate celebration for the 100th anniversary of Abraham Lincoln's birth in February of 1909. Not only was Susan very involved in the planning and implementation process, but she also hosted several national DAR officers in her home for the occasion.[14] She served on many committees and frequently welcomed DAR members for meetings in her home. One project that she shepherded was the design and placement of a plaque on the Court House square that listed the names of the men who served in the American Revolutionary War and are buried in Sangamon County.

Installed in 1911, the plaque is still on the Old State Capitol Square in Springfield, attached to the north wall of the plaza kiosk.

DAR Plaque
Carl Volkmann

Her roles as community philanthropist and volunteer were dwarfed by the many social engagements she engineered. The parties in the Lawrence House varied. Newspapers reported intimate luncheons in the dining room and tented parties in the garden with 1,000 guests.[15] Over 100 Chicago suffragettes who were visiting the state capital were welcomed at a reception. The guest list of that party included Jane Addams of Hull House fame.[16] All of Susan's parties were tastefully decorated with coordinated colors and fresh flowers. Many of Susan's out-of-town guests stayed with her, presumably in the smaller house across Third Street. Her local guests were the cream of Springfield society. Governor and Mrs. Deneen frequently attended Susan's galas.

Christmas time was a special occasion at the Lawrence House. The Christmas celebration of 1906 was equally as elaborate as the 1905 housewarming celebration but of a totally different nature. Lasting from December 24 to January 4, the luncheons, card parties, dinners, receptions, and trips to the opera house were all planned to honor Susan's several out-of-town house guests.[17] The DAR membership was lavishly entertained at a special Christmas party with a colonial theme in 1908. A reporter described the decorations:

> Christmas greens, the holly wreaths, and the red Christmas bells were used effectively throughout the spacious home. In the living room the windows were decorated with California peppers and holly wreaths were hung in all of the windows. The quaint large fireplace in the hall was completely surrounded with holly. To enhance the beauty of this, the balcony just opposite was hung with the folds of the American flag together with wreaths of laurel and mistletoe. The fountain was beautifully adorned with red and white carnations. . . In the center of the large table was a Christmas tree elaborately trimmed with tinseled ornaments and colonial bells. Beautiful mats of lace were laid on the tables and silken candelabra gave forth a subdued light. . .
>
> Entertainment for the guests was provided by the choir of Christ Church, readings in the 'colonial style' by Miss Margaret Brooks, and the playing of plantation melodies by three colored men, two of whom were

slaves in Missouri. The instruments used were a banjo, guitar and violin, which were furnished by Mrs. Dana.[18]

Christmas Greeting from Susan
Dana-Thomas House Archives

References in her spirit letters indicate that the widowed Susan had several suitors during that time. Dr. H. H. Tuttle of Riverton, Illinois, seemed to be a viable candidate for marriage. In her spirit letters, Susan asked her parents time and again if she should marry Dr. Tuttle despite the fact that she did not love him, and time and again they encouraged her to follow her heart. Tuttle was an old friend of the family. An honorary pall bearer at Mary's funeral, he had studied medicine and surgery in Berlin, Heidelberg, and Vienna.[19] Perhaps in an effort to solve the marriage dilemma, Susan brought Tuttle to a sitting with Mrs. Pruden, the medium from Cincinnati. The results were not only a spirit letter from Susan's mother but also spirit letters from Tuttle's mother who was also "on the other side." Mary's letter assured the doctor that he was treating Susie correctly, and that she would soon be well and strong again. Mrs. Tuttle declared her love for her son and forecast some future events in his life. Both avoided the marriage issue.[20] Susan must have followed her heart, because a neighbor across the street from the Lawrence House recalled that she saw the handsome Dr. Tuttle come to Susan's front door to call on her with a large bouquet of flowers. Shortly after he was welcomed into the house, the door opened again and "...out he flew. Then came the roses."[21]

The doctor recovered. He married and distinguished himself in World War I. Tuttle organized and trained the medical detachments of the 130th infantry, 33rd division and the 123rd and 124th machine gun battalion. Dubbed "Tuttle's Unit," the men were instructed in anatomy, first aid, nursing, dispensary work, litter bearing, and x-ray operation at St. John's Hospital in Springfield. Their military training took place at the Springfield arsenal. All units served on the front lines in Europe.[22]

Despite her demanding schedule, Susan found time to travel extensively. The newspapers chronicled her continuing domestic trips, and in 1907 she took a six-month tour of Europe with two friends and a cousin. *Kaiser Wilhelm de Grosse*, the vessel on which she traveled, was state of the art. It was launched 10 years before Susan sailed and was the pride of Germany. The first liner to have a wireless telegraphy system, the ship could carry 1,506 passengers and cross the Atlantic in less than six days. Like rail travel, trans-Atlantic sailing on a luxury liner was a relatively new phenomenon. In what was called the golden age of ocean liners, companies competed for wealthy passengers who sought speed, comfort, and luxury between America and Europe. Like the *Lusitania* (a ship Susan sailed on at a later date), *Kaiser Wilhelm* was destined to have a bleak place in history. Seven years after Susan's trip, World War I broke out, and the ship was converted by the German government to a high speed merchant cruiser. Within weeks after war was declared, a British warship sunk her.[23] Susan traveled to Europe with her friend Celia Hughes for three months in 1908 on another historic German ship, the SS *Amerika*. Launched in 1905, this larger and newer ship carried 2,508 passengers. The ship's last voyage on the Hamburg-Boulogne-Southampton-Boston route was July 14, 1914, and in April of 1917 she was seized by the United States, renamed "*America*," and became a U.S. Army transport ship. In 1917-18 she made nine voyages to France with American troops.[24]

*Art Glass Butterflies over
Entrance of Lawrence House*
Virginia Scott

Susan seemed to personify the butterflies that adorned her home during that time. She wore one-of-a-kind gowns made by Springfield's finest seamstresses as she soared from board meetings to parties to Europe. Yet the woman who was on the edges of history and at the top of Springfield society had many dark moments during that period. Two of her closest friends died. Celia Hughes, the medium from Chicago who went to Europe with Susan on her 1908 trip,[25] passed away on March 10, 1909.[26] Leigh Gross Day, a close friend from childhood, died of Bright's disease on May 26, 1910 at the early age of 49.[27] Furthermore, Susan again had several bouts with ill health. She explained in a 1914 letter to a friend that she was subject to bronchial colds, and when she coughed, she would severely hemorrhage from her nose. Doctors had to operate on her nose in March of 1911 to stop the hemorrhages.[28] Beneath Susan's colorful public persona was an insecure woman who had suffered much personal tragedy. The butterfly at the Lawrence House always seemed to have a cloud of adversity hovering around her.

Notes from Chapter 9:

1. "Society is interested," *Illinois State Journal,* June 28, 1905, p. 5.
2. "Society," *Springfield News,* January 5, 1907, p.3.
3. "Play will be social event," *Illinois State Journal,* May 17, 1908, p. 6.
4. "Organ recital will be given," *Illinois State Journal,* July 12, 1908, p. 6.
5. "Society," *Illinois State Journal,* April 7, 1911, p. 7.
6. Ibid., May 7, 1911, p. 10
7. "Many to see opera tonight," *Illinois State Journal,* January 19, 1912, p. 7.
8. "Humane society elects officers," *Illinois State Journal,* January17, 1909, p. 5.
9. "King's daughters' circles meet," *Illinois State Journal,* April 29, 1908, p. 6.
10. "Georg to Talk on Photography," *Illinois State Journal,* November 5, 1909, p. 12.
11. "Specimens of art please critical," *Illinois State Journal,* May 3, 1911, p. 12.
12. "Mrs. Susan Lawrence Dana hostess," *Illinois State Journal*, October 15, 1909, p. 6.
13. "Architect talks on city beautiful" *Illinois State Journal,* April 25, 1906, p. 4.
14. "Nation's leading matrons here for D.A.R reception," *Illinois State Journal,* February 12, 1909, p.1.
15. "Is hostess at brilliant party," *Illinois State Journal* June 23, 1906, p. 6.
16. "Mrs. Dana entertains suffragists," *Illinois State Journal*, April 14, 1909, p. 6.
17. "Socially speaking," *Springfield News,* December 24, 1906, p. 3.
18. "Daughters of revolution meet," *Illinois State Journal,* December 27, 1908, p. 6.
19. "City and vicinity," *Illinois State Journal*, March 9, 1899, p. 6.
20. Spirit Letters, Box 1, Folder 15, Dana Bice Collection.
21. Gertrude Mathias Durkin, interviewed by Richard Taylor and Regina McGuire, October, 1984, transcript in Dana-Thomas House Archives.
22. Duff, Nellie Brown, *The Honor Book, Sangamon County, Illinois 1917-19* A.P. (Illiopolis, Illinois:Bickenback, 1920), p. 44.
23. http://www.lostliners.com/Kaisergrosse.html
24. http://www.roangelo.net/angelo/amerika.html
25. Jennie Willits to Susan Dana, March 18, 1909, Box 1 ½, Folder 2, Dana Bice Collection.
26. "Embalming delayed," *The Republican-Register*, March 10, 1909, p. 1.
27. "Mrs. George E. Day, artist, is called," *Illinois State Journal*, May 27, 1910, p. 6.
28. Susan Lawrence Joergen-Dahl to Samuel Fallows, March 2, 1914, Samuel Fallows Papers, State Historical Society of Wisconsin.

10

Mrs. Lawrence Joergen-Dahl (Dede): Bride Again

It was another lovely luncheon at the Lawrence House. The February 13, 1912, newspaper announced that Susan Lawrence Dana would be hosting a Valentine's Day musicale for Governor and Mrs. Deneen at which a noted Chicago baritone, "George Vahl," would be singing.[1] The next day the newspaper reviewed the recital and luncheon under the headline, "Joergen 'Dohl,' Noted Baritone and Local Talent, Participate in Program—Governor and Mrs. Deneen Present." According to the reporter, the musicians who entertained the guests were "Goergen Dahl," baritone of the Columbia School of Music in Chicago, and Miss Theoline Pohlson, Springfield violinist. Vernor Henshie, pianist, accompanied them both. As usual, the Lawrence House was appropriately decorated for the holiday:

> Valentine symbols were employed with leading hearts and hyacinths forming a generous portion. Specially prominent were these flowers in the music room. Palms and ferns furnished the banking scheme of the music room balcony. Pale pink was used in the drawing room. In the luncheon, a general heart scheme was followed.[2]

What the newspaper did not report was that the love theme had special significance because Susan was using the occasion to introduce Joergen Dahl, her new romantic interest, to her Springfield friends. Eventually the two married, and his hyphenated name, Joergen-Dahl, became Susan's surname. The local press learned to spell it correctly.

Susan and Joergen met sometime in 1911 at the Chicago home of Mrs. J. Kjellberg, a mutual friend. The handsome young Dane was teaching voice at the Columbia School of Music in Chicago while launching a promising career as a professional singer. Joergen received rave reviews for his solo work with the Chicago Mendelssohn Club, a prestigious 60 voice male glee club, and had contracted with the Briggs Musical Bureau to manage his career. He sang regularly at the Oak Park Christian Science Church.[3]

Young Joergen Dahl
Dana-Thomas House Archives

Joergen Constantin Dahl was born to a prominent family on November 1, 1886, in Struer, Denmark. His father was inspector of the posts (similar to this country's postmaster general). His uncle owned the largest newspaper in Denmark and was president of the European international press bureau. Joergen had one sister. In 1907 he received a grant from the Danish government to come to the United States to gain "commercial knowledge," and in 1910 he signed a contract with the First National Bank of Milwaukee to learn the banking business. Commercial knowledge apparently did not suit the young Dane because in 1911 he signed a contract with Columbia College to teach voice.

It was a whirlwind romance. A month after the Valentine party Susan wrote a confidential letter to her cousin Flora announcing her intention to marry the 26 year old Joergen in Philadelphia, justifying her decision, and asking Flora to be a witness for the event. Susan's own words answered some of the questions Flora surely had.

Will the age difference present problems?

I do not have any apprehension as to the difference in ages be a menace to our congeniality. I am young in tastes—he is old in his own understanding of life as the same. . . If I am ever going to consider marriage, I feel it is the thing to do now. I would not want to deprive any man from the privilege of having a child if they wanted it. It would at least make them content to realize whether they had one or not. That they could do so if they desired to.[4]

Why Philadelphia?

We have looked up the question of New York City license—am told that none is required. Therefore have decided not to try this for two reasons—we do not want the license in a New York paper and do not want any question of no license to ever come up. We want it all a matter of record that any one may look up. When the time comes for it to be known, some busy body will look it up, so we have decided to stop in Philadelphia where the license is iron-clad and the papers have a less general circulation—and the notice of the license will not be as readily seen. We want no question about anything that anyone could criticize—the stir of a quick marriage for our own reasons—and the difference of age—would make quite stir enough.[5]

Why the secrecy?

Both of us are of one mind in regard to all this—for business reasons on both sides, we do not want anyone at present to know we are married. . .He says his parents are of such a retiring nature, he would rather go home to see them this summer and tell them then.[6]

46

Susan and Joergen
Dana-Thomas House Archives

The couple was married by Reverend William Chalfont at the Thirteenth Street Methodist Church in Philadelphia on March 19, 1912. The marriage license listed the groom's age as 26 and the bride's age as 36. Susan was actually 49 years old. Joergen changed his first name to Lawrence, and they both assumed Joergen-Dahl as their last name.

Susan had reinvented herself again. In a complete role reversal contrary to the standards ingrained in her, she was supporting a man. Lawrence was earning very little money and had a debt to the Danish government for the contract which he had not fulfilled. Possibly he was even facing deportation. Susan's money could rescue him. The official marriage license which she referred to in her letter to Flora assured that as her husband, Lawrence could remain in the United States to cultivate his budding career. He was, however, more than a protégé. Susan felt that through the relationship she regained her youth and found a soul mate. She wrote in her letter to Flora:

> I find in him qualities that I have never found in another man. The clear crystal purity of atmosphere, his high ideals, his artistic nature, and his ability to forge ahead—all interest and appeal to me. . .Our understanding of life is the same. His nature is most sweet and lovable. His devotion and love for sure is beautiful and sincere.[7]

The date for the wedding was chosen because Lawrence had an audition in New York with Victrola Records.[8] After their trip east, the new Mr. and Mrs. Lawrence Joergen-Dahl returned briefly to Chicago and then came back to Springfield where Susan prepared for their European honeymoon. On May 14, 1912, the couple sailed from Boston to Liverpool aboard the Cunard *S.S. Franconia I*, a short-lived luxury liner that was launched in 1910, requisitioned as a World War I troop ship in 1915, and torpedoed by the Germans in 1916.[9] While they were in Europe, Lawrence studied music, and the couple visited his family at their home in Renders, Denmark, toured the continent, and shopped. Among Susan's purchases was an elaborate baby layette which she undoubtedly hoped to use for the children she would bear. Tragically, all of the unused baby clothes were sold at an auction of Susan's possessions near the end of her life. A christening gown with the French price tag still attached is preserved in the archives of the State of Illinois owned Dana-Thomas House.

The couple returned to Springfield on December 1, 1912, for the social season and then returned to Europe in early 1913. A letter dated February 13, 1913, from Lawrence to Susan (his dearest Dede) reveals that Susan was traveling in Europe alone while he was with his parents at their home in Denmark, and once again Susan suffered from a debilitating illness. This time it was a cold which prevented her from going to London.[10]

When Mr. and Mrs. Joergen-Dahl returned to Springfield on March 27,[11] they plunged into the social, civic, artistic, and charitable worlds of the city. The day after they returned, Mrs. George Sanders hosted a tea for the Mary Lawrence Circle of the King's Daughters to honor the new bride. Susan was given a silver tray.[12] Under the auspices of the Amateur Musical Club, Lawrence presented a well-received joint concert with pianist Sarah Suttel at the First Presbyterian Church on April 17.[13] He presented several private recitals at the Lawrence House. Susan was a patroness of a benefit musical presented by the Woman's Club for the Tuberculosis Society,[14] a hostess at the Governor's mansion for a reception given by Governor Dunne's wife and daughters,[15] and a member of the local reception committee for the American Association of Officials of Charity and Corrections which met for three days at the St. Nicholas Hotel in June of 1913.[16]

On May 9, 1913, Lawrence sang at the "Illinois Half Century Freedom Exposition" at the Lincoln Colored Home (then called the Old Folks and Orphans Home). Governor Edward F. Dunne and a former minister to Haiti were speakers for the occasion. The purpose of the event was to celebrate the anniversary of the home as well as to generate interest in pending legislation that proposed a 1915 statewide exposition to acknowledge 50 years of Negro emancipation.[17]

The legislation passed In June 1913, and House Bill 919 created the eight member Illinois Commission Half-Century Anniversary of Negro Freedom with a $25,000 appropriation to "arrange for and conduct during the year 1915 at a place to be selected by said commission, an exhibition and celebration to commemorate the fiftieth anniversary of the freeing of the Negro from slavery."[18] Susan Lawrence Joergen-Dahl was the only woman appointed by Governor Dunne to the Commission. She was elected vice-president of the group, and her friend Reverend Samuel Fallows was elected president. The commission hired staff and leased office space in Chicago as it began plans for a 1915 commemorative celebration.[19] Susan had attained what she was seeking since her spirit letters to her father—an opportunity to serve in the public arena.

Notes for Chapter 10:

1. "Mrs. Dana will entertain," *Illinois State Journal,* February 13, 1912, p. 9.
2. "Valentine musical is pretty event," *Illinois State* Journal, February 14, 1912, p. 9.
3. Joergen-Dahl papers, box 11/2, Folder 4. Dana Bice Collection.
4. Susan Lawrence Dana to Cousin Flora, box 11/2, Folder 3, Dana Bice Collection.
5. Ibid.
6. Ibid.
7. Ibid.
8. Ibid.
9. http://www.gjenvick.com/HistoricalBrochures/Steamships-OceanLiners/CunardLine/1912-RMS-FranconiaAndLaconia.html
10. Joergen-Dahl papers, box 11/2, Folder 4, Dana Bice Collection.
11. "Mrs. George A. Sanders hostess," *Illinois State Journal,* March 28, 1913, p. 8.
12. "King's daughters entertain," *Illinois State Journal,* March 29, 1913, p. 9.
13. "Success attends club's recital," *Illinois State Journal*, April 18, 1913, p. 7.
14. "Big crowd greets princess bonnie," *Illinois State Journal*, May 23, 1913, p. 9.
15. "Pretty affair is held at mansion," *Illinois State Journal,* May 29, 1913, p. 9.
16. "Program complete for charity meet," *Illinois State Journal,* May 31, 1913, p. 10.
17. "Negroes to hear Governor Dunne," *Illinois State Journal,* May 9, 1913, p. 1.
18. House Bill 919, *History and Report of the Exhibition And Celebration to Commemorate the Fifteenth Anniversary of the Emancipation of the Negro,* (Chicago:Fraternal Press, 1914).
19. Letter dated September 6, 1913, Fallows Collection, Wisconsin Historical Society Archives.

11

Mrs. Lawrence Joergen-Dahl: Widow Again

On Wednesday, July 16, 1913, Susan and Lawrence took the train to Chicago. She was to attend the first meeting of the Illinois Commission Half-Century Anniversary of Negro Freedom, and he had meetings with other musicians scheduled. On Thursday they went to Highland Park where they visited former Governor and Mrs. Deneen until Saturday morning when they returned to Chicago. They attended services at Bishop Fallows' church on Sunday morning and went to the home of Ida King in Oak Park that afternoon. Lawrence and Miss King spent the evening selecting songs for his winter concerts. When Susan and Lawrence took the train back to Chicago, he complained of chills and a slight headache.

After a day of business engagements on Monday, the couple went to the home of Mr. and Mrs. Graves, friends on the south side of Chicago, for dinner. Since her husband was still not feeling well, Susan borrowed a thermometer, and Lawrence had a 101 degree temperature. When Susan treated him in the room at the Hotel Sherman with various remedies, his temperature returned to normal, but on Tuesday afternoon, the fever returned. Susan sent for a doctor who treated him for a cold. Although Lawrence stayed in bed Wednesday morning (continuing to sing), his temperature again spiked. After the doctor saw him at the hotel again, Lawrence was moved by ambulance at Susan's request to the home of Mrs. Kjellberg (where Susan and Lawrence met). Susan chose to attend to him herself rather than take him to a hospital. They arrived at the Kjellberg home about 6:30 p.m. on Wednesday evening. Despite the fact that specialists were called, Lawrence's condition continued to deteriorate. At one point his temperature was 106 degrees. The doctors performed several tests and determined that he was suffering from acute Bright's disease, an inflammation of the kidneys called nephritis today. Ironically, that was the same disease that took the life of Susan's childhood friend, Leigh Gross Day. Lawrence Joergen-Dahl died on Saturday evening, July 26, 1913, with Susan at his side.

Once again Susan took a deceased loved one back to the Lawrence House and to eventual rest in Oak Ridge Cemetery. Two Chicago friends accompanied her on this train trip. After only 16 months of marriage, Susan was again a widow.

With her usual dramatic flair, Susan greeted guests who came to the visitation preceding the funeral services for Lawrence with her arms full of roses and with recordings of Lawrence singing in the background.[1] The coffin rested in the Lawrence House gallery and was surrounded by lilies and roses. The Danish and American flags crossed on the top.

Two funeral services were conducted on the afternoon of July 29. The first was held at noon for members of the African-American community "as a mark of respect for the many kind deeds done and assistance rendered their race by the Joergen-Dahls." Newspaper reports of attendance at that service vary from 300 to 800. An Episcopal service took place at three o'clock. Special music was provided by Vernon Henshle (Lawrence's accompanist at the Amateur Musical recital), piano, John Taylor, violin, and George Koehn, flute. Attendees from out of town included Denmark Consul Beck, Chicago; Mr. and Mrs. Axel Fabriansen, now of Chicago, formerly of Renders, Denmark; Mr. and Mrs. F.S. Kjellberg of Chicago; Mrs. W.O. Graves, Chicago; Mrs. George R. Anthony, Detroit, Michigan; Mr and Mrs. Charles Messerly, Sedalia, Missouri; Miss Jennie Wyckoff, Lincoln; R.N. Lawrence, Lincoln; W. Lawrence, Atlanta.[2]

Both services were conducted by Bishop Samuel Fallows of Chicago. Thomas Wallace Swann, a Springfield African-American activist, also spoke at the noon service. Both men were members with Susan of the Half Century Commission. Bishop Fallows was no ordinary churchman. During his 78 years he served as a Civil War soldier, clergyman, civic leader, educator, reformer, and patriot. Ordained a Methodist minister, Fallows held varied positions of leadership including superintendent of public instruction in Wisconsin, president of Illinois Wesleyan University at Bloomington, Illinois, president and presiding bishop of the Reformed Episcopal Church, president of the Board of Managers of the Illinois State Reformatory at Pontiac, Illinois, and a national officer in the Grand Army of the Republic (GAR).[3]

Bishop Fallows paid tribute to both Susan and Lawrence in his remarks. He said of Lawrence, "He was a singer possessing rarest qualities of voice and expression. I had learned to love him deeply for his estimable personal qualities, for his amiability and for his readiness to help others, involving very often the sacrifice of his own ease, comfort and time." After noting Susan's philanthropic work and her influence among women and the African-American community, he concluded, "She found in Mr. Dahl a sympathetic and enthusiastic supporter. Their married life was a dream of beauty and useful helpfulness."[4]

After Lawrence's death, Susan again turned to spirit letters for more assurance and comfort. In a letter to her late husband, she asked how it felt to die, if she was caring for his things as he would wish, if she should tell his family about their communications, and if she should continue serving on the Commission for Half-Century Anniversary of Negro Freedom Celebration. The letter was signed "Your loving dovebird, Dede Buss." Like the spirit letters from her father and mother, Lawrence's replies were positive and encouraging:

> "I have discovered that death is not the end of life but an event in life."
> "You did with all of my things just what I wanted done with them."
> "Do not hesitate to tell my dear people that you have heard from me."
> "I think you better go on with the Commission work."[5]

Susan took his advice and immersed herself in the business of the commission for six months. The task of planning such a celebration was not easy. As vice-president, Susan worked closely with the chair, Bishop Fallows. The correspondence between them reveals that the commission struggled with the classic Chicago-downstate disagreements, financial conflicts, and personnel controversies. The minutes of the executive committee meetings reflected Susan's insightful and constructive contributions to the process. She was of special value to the group because of her access to the governor. She traveled extensively on commission business.

In a letter dated February 26, 1914, Susan indicated to Bishop Fallows that she was bedridden with a serious cold. At this point in her life, Susan was struck down with severe colds almost every February or March. During the month of March she continued to work on commission business from her home. Her condition, a combination of exhaustion, severe stress, and

Mrs. Susan Lawrence Joergen-Dahl
Dana-Thomas House Archives

her chronic cold and hemorrhage affliction, deteriorated. Additionally, her cousin Flora became ill, and with only temporary help in the house, Susan cared for her. On March 31, 1914, under doctor's orders, Susan regretfully resigned from the Illinois Commission Half-Century Anniversary of Negro Freedom.[6]

The happy bride who had at last found a way to serve society was replaced by a frail widow who was too weak to leave her home. Once more Susan would need the inner strength and resiliency that had served her so well in the past as, at age 51, she still strove to find her place in the world.

Notes for Chapter 11:

1. Charlotte Ide Jess, interviewed by Richard Taylor and Regina McGuire, September, 1984, transcript in Dana-Thomas collection.
2. "Churchman gives praise to Dane," *Illinois State Journal*, July 30, 1913, p. 8.
3. http://www.wisconsinhistory.org/dictionary/index.asp?action=view&term=1279&keyword=fallows
4. "Churchman gives praise to Dane," *Illinois State Journal*, July 30, 1913, p. 8.
5. Spirit Letters, Box 1, Folder 15, Dana Bice Collection.
6. Susan Joergen-Dahl to Bishop Fallows, March 13, 1914, Fallows Collection, Wisconsin Historical Society Archives.

12

Mrs. Charles Lawrence-Gehrmann: Partner

Susan remained cloistered in the Lawrence House for the last half of 1913 and most of 1914. Her whole world was collapsing around her. While Europe, her frequent playground, was about to break into World War I, Susan was nursing her cousin Flora back to health and trying to regain her own strength. The resiliency she had mustered in the past did not come easily this time. She began to re-emerge into society when, in November of 1914, she addressed a meeting of Springfield's African-American citizens encouraging them to participate in an exhibition to be held at the state armory.[1] By the first of January, 1915, she was able to assist at the annual governor's wife's reception at the Governor's Mansion.[2] In early February Susan sought relief in a warmer climate by visiting her cousin in Oakland, California. However, she still suffered from stomach problems while she was there.

Sometime during this vulnerable period of Susan's life, she re-united with Springfield native Charles Gehrmann. As childhood friends, Susan and Charles attended primary school together at the Bettie Stuart Institute. It is unclear where and when they met again although one newspaper account reports that Charles was in Springfield during the Christmas holiday in 1913. Bishop Fallows, who had remained her confidant on personal matters, was the first of Susan's friends to receive the startling news. In a letter to him dated February 22, 1915, Susan wrote, "I have been in this western country only two weeks, which seems short in one sense of the word, but in this case of it has proven sufficiently long enough for me to make up my mind. I am going to get married here. . .Am marrying Mr. Charles A. Gehrmann. . .My one regret being married out here is that we cannot be married by you. I would so love to have you perform the ceremony."[3]

Charles was one of five children of Minnie and Charles A. Gehrmann, a German immigrant who owned a successful dry goods store at 118 South Fifth Street in Springfield. The Gehrmann and Lawrence families were close friends. The senior Gehrmann served on the Springfield School Board with Susan's father Rheuna. The boyhood home of Charles at 1021 North Third Street was as renowned in Springfield as the Lawrence House but in quite a different way. The large red brick traditional house was surrounded by formal gardens with ornate fountains, statuary, and carved birdbaths. Two tennis courts and a large conservatory were on the three acres of ground. Ironically, all the elaborate furnishings of the house were sold at a large auction just a year after Susan's possessions were sold at auction.[4] In 1945 the property was given to the city of Springfield by the surviving cousin of Charles, and a park which remains today between North Second and North Third Streets was developed.[5]

Parents and Youngest Siblings of Charles in Family Garden (1882)
Sangamon Valley Collection

After graduating from Springfield High School, Charles left Springfield in 1883 for Golden, Colorado, where he attended the Colorado School of Mines. He graduated in 1886 with a Bachelor of Science degree in chemistry.[6] By 1890 Charles was established as a promising young citizen of Idaho Springs, Colorado. He was elected secretary of the Board of Directors of the Idaho Springs School District by an overwhelming majority. The *Idaho Springs News* called him "active, intelligent and enterprising, and in every way qualified for the duties he will be called upon to perform."[7] The social life and travels of Charles and his wife were chronicled extensively by the newspaper. The couple frequently hosted guests from central Illinois. By 1892 the newspaper was lauding Charles's abilities as manager of the Salisbury, Stanley, and Hukill mines.[8]

His career at Idaho Springs was cut short, however, when he facilitated the sale of the Stanley Mine to a group of Montreal businessmen. Because of a number of contentious issues, a prolonged court battle among Charles, the other stockholders of the Stanley Company, and the Canadian buyers resulted in the shutdown of the mine.[9] Then, after a long struggle with sciatic rheumatism, the first Mrs. Gehrmann (nee Jennie Belmore) died on June 3, 1895.[10] At some point Charles married again. That marriage ended in divorce in Reno, Nevada, in 1910.[11]

From all reports, the professional life of Charles was diverse. According to Susan's letter to Bishop Fallows, he was a trained mining engineer and "an analytical and physiological chemist, Dr. of science, philosophy and medicine. . .[who held] many honorary degrees for special work."[12] His obituary stated that he designed an original flume to carry water down a mountainside to furnish power for a mine and a method to control landslides which was adopted by engineers who were building the Panama Canal.

The obituary also noted that he was president of a Rawhide, Nevada, bank.[13] Rawhide was a mining town that sprang up in the Nevada desert in 1908. According to the *New York Times*, after the discovery of gold in the nearby hills, as many as 150 people poured into the town daily. Most of them were investors who came from Reno in that new invention, the automobile, and were seeking easy wealth. Within three months, eight banks, four newspapers, and enumerable lodging houses were built.[14] Charles was at the center of that rush. As president of one of those banks, he shared his geological observations of Rawhide's mines with citizens of Reno and encouraged them to take advantage of the opportunities.[15] However, the dreams of Charles and every other speculator did not materialize. Due to a disastrous fire and, most importantly, a shortage of gold, the rush was short-lived. Rawhide boasted a population of 7,000 in June of 1908, and had only 500 citizens in 1910.[16]

The wedding of Susan and Charles was held on February 27, 1915, in the home of Susan's cousin, Mrs. George Davis, in Oakland, California. Susan said she was 44 and Charles claimed to be 49 on the marriage license.[17] (They were actually 52 and 53 respectively.) Charles changed his name to Charles Lawrence Gehrmann. At the beginning of the marriage, they seemed to be compatible. Susan expressed a deep respect for him in a letter to Anna Lloyd Jones Wright (Frank Lloyd Wright's mother) written in 1917:

Mr. Charles Augustus Gehrmann
Mrs. Susan Lawrence Joergen-Dahl
Married
on Saturday, the twenty-seventh day of February
one thousand nine hundred and fifteen
Oakland, California

Marriage Announcement
Dana Bice Collection

> He is a fine man. In his great simplicity lies all there is of greatness. I find much
> pleasure and comfort in his perfect companionship. He has such a fine mind which had had
> thorough scientific training. His disposition is perfect. It is a joy to meet and associate with one
> so poised and perfectly balanced.[18]

They were business partners. She still owned mining properties in the West, and he had mining expertise. In the letter to Mrs. Wright, Susan wrote, ". . .we are opening up a large gold property which so far promises to yield us large returns for our time and capital invested. It is due to us both that we got some return soon, for all the failures of the last few years."[19] Springfield and the Lawrence House were no longer the center of Susan's life. The couple led an itinerant life style. Together they pursued many of Charles's business schemes and were seen at social events in many American cities. Their address was frequently a hotel. The letter to Mrs. Wright was written from a New York City apartment where Susan wrote that during the first half of 1917 they were in St. Louis,

New York, and Washington, D.C. (where they attended events celebrating the inauguration of Woodrow Wilson).[20] After they returned to Springfield for three weeks that year, Charles went to Oatman, Arizona, and Susan went to Chicago, Battle Creek, and Detroit, Michigan.[21]

Susan had changed her persona once more. She replaced the art-centered life she had enjoyed with Lawrence with the adventurous business world of Charles.

Notes for Chapter 12:

1. "Colored persons aid survey show," *Illinois State Journal,* November 16, 1914, p. 2.
2. "Hundreds received at mansion affair," *Illinois State Journal,* January 2, 1915, p. 8.
3. Susan Joergen-Dahl to Bishop Fallows, February 22, 1915, Fallows Collection, Wisconsin Historical Society Archives.
4. "Out of the past," *Illinois State Journal,* June 25, 1944.
5. Gehrmann Biography, SVC.
6. *Catalogue of the State School of Mines, 1885-86* (Golden, Colorado: Golden Globe Power Printer, 1886), P. 14.
7. "Won educational honors," *Illinois State Journal,* May 16, 1890, p. 4.
8. *Idaho Springs News,* July 1, 1892.
9. "Stanley trouble" *Denver Times,* March 3, 1901, p. 3.
10. Obituaries, *Idaho Springs News,* June 7, 1895.
11. "Surprise is made with marriage license," *Oakland Tribune,* February 27, 1915. p. 2.
12. Susan Joergen-Dahl to Bishop Fallows, February 28, 1915, Fallows Collection, Wisconsin Historical Society Archives.
13. "Dr. C. A. Gehrmann claimed by death," *State Journal Register,* May 21, 1944, p. 10.
14. *"Romance and reality in the rush to Rawhide,"* *New York Times,* June 21, 1908, p. PSM10.
15. *"Colonel Gehrman, mining expert, talks of Rawhide,"* *Nevada State Journal,* March 2, 1908, p. 6.
16. *"Romance and reality in the rush to Rawhide,"* *New York Times,* June 21, 1908, p. PSM10.
17. "Surprise is made with marriage license," *Oakland Tribune,* February 27, 1915. p. 2.
18. Susan Lawrence-Gehrmann to Anne Lloyd Jones Wright, July 29, 1917, Dana-Thomas archives.
19. Ibid.
20. *"Society," Washington Post* March 4, 1917, p. E2.
21. Susan Lawrence-Gehrmann to Anne Lloyd Jones Wright, July 29, 1917, Dana-Thomas archives.

13

Susan Lawrence-Gehrmann: Divorcee

By 1920 the marriage of Susan and Charles was failing. Susan said in a letter to her cousin Marie Georgia Jefferson, "We never had a word of disagreement in our lives. Just an unfortunate number of circumstances caused us to drift apart."[1] The primary unfortunate circumstance was undoubtedly a bill of complaint filed against Charles Lawrence Gehrmann in Sangamon County, Illinois Circuit Court in May, 1919, by Lilian M. Grahame, a music teacher from Denver, Colorado. In the complaint Lilian claimed that although Charles had been a resident of Springfield, Illinois, for the past two years, he had not lived in one place longer than a few weeks before that time. According to her, he moved from state to state "Engaged as a solicitor and promoter of various fraudulent mining and agricultural projects." Furthermore, he deceitfully professed for twenty years "to be an expert in western mining and agricultural industries and has thus advertised himself to those with whom he came in contact."[2]

According to the bill of complaint, Charles and Lilian met in April of 1905 when Charles "protested his love, affection, and admiration for [her]." Trusting in that love, Lilian sent $1,000 on January 25, 1907, to Charles in Goldfield, Nevada, for investment in a mine. Charles promised her he would "personally guarantee her against loss of any kind." She was never able to get an accounting of that money. On October 1, 1910, after Charles' divorce from his second wife, the couple became engaged. Over the next two years Charles induced Lilian to buy tracts of land in California from J. Nelson Watt. According to Charles, the lands would be valuable in the future for the cultivation of eucalyptus trees. "To insure the future welfare and happiness of both defendant and complainant when they should become united in marriage. . .[Charles] earnestly and urgently insisted on the purchase of at least three tracts of said land by [Lillian]." She sent $3,000 to Charles in California in various payments in 1911. After investigation, Lilian discovered that the land was worthless, and Charles and J. Nelson Watt had fraudulently sold parcels to a large number of other people. All the money Lilian sent to Charles was lost.

Lilian did not see or hear from Charles from September 1913 to September 1917 when "by diligent effort and at a great expense and after much mental anguish and suffering, [she] finally discovered that [Charles] was alive and that his home was in Springfield, Illinois, and that in violation of his promise to marry [Lilian], he had married another woman named Susan Lawrence Dana." After trying with no success to "come to a settlement, account and adjustment" out of court, Lilian was requesting that Charles be summoned to court .[3]

On March 20, 1919, the Sangamon County sheriff knocked on the door of the Lawrence House. Susan answered the door, The sheriff handed her a summons for Charles to appear in court and informed her of the contents of that summons.[4] Charles did not respond to Lilian's claims. Rather, in May Charles filed a plea in abatement claiming that at the time the summons was served, he was a resident of Oatman, Arizona, and that during his married life he had never been a resident of the Lawrence House in Springfield, Sangamon County, or the state of Illinois.[5]

A series of court-ordered depositions was conducted in Oatman, Arizona, to prove that Charles was a resident there. Testimony was given by J. H. Drake, owner of the Arizona Hotel where Charles purportedly lived; J .J. McCarthy, business partner of Charles who claimed to have moved from Reno to Oatman with Charles to develop a mine; John M. Hines, Jr., deputy sheriff; Lee R. Meyers, another business partner; Wilbur A. Brooks, a friend; Louis L. Wallace, attorney; and Charles. Charles testified:

> When the question of being married first came up, I explained to [my wife] that my interests were all in the West and that her interests were all in the East, that I could not afford to be married unless I could take care of my interests in the West; that I would not wish to go to Springfield, Illinois, under any circumstances. . .She consented to this arrangement and we decided to keep our interests absolutely separate and to join each other at such places and times when our business interests permitted.[6]

Attorney Louis Wallace clarified the issue in this exchange:

> Question: Mr. Wallace, is it not a fact that it is impossible for a wife to disclaim the residence of her husband and not the husband of the wife unless there is an agreement to that effect?
> Wallace: I believe that is correct.
> Question: In other words the residence of the husband as the head of the family is the residence and the household of the family?
> Wallace: Yes sir.

After denying repeatedly that he was a resident of Springfield since he was married, Charles was cross examined by Lillian's attorney with these questions:

> Dr. Gehrmann, were you the administrator of your father's estate in the Courts of Sangamon County, Illinois?

Dr. do you not know the laws of Illinois require every administrator to be a resident and citizen of the State of Illinois?

Did you not take an oath in the administration proceedings connected with your father's estate that you were a resident and citizen in the State of Illinois?

As an administrator of your father's estate were you not required to be in Springfield, Illinois, during the course of that administration procedure?

When did you close your father's estate?[7]

To avoid perjuring himself, Charles refused to answer any of those questions. The final document from this case was a motion filed June 2, 1920, by Lilian's attorney to suppress the deposition of Charles on the grounds that he was unresponsive. Since no other record of further court action existed, the case was undoubtedly settled out of court at a great cost to Susan.

The couple was estranged for the next 10 years. After experiencing a good deal of emotional and financial trauma, Susan decided to terminate the relationship. She sent a letter to Charles on September 19, 1930 that said:

I can no longer proceed under the negative conditions of our relationship. The strain is most detrimental to me and must be terminated. Since May 1920 D'Arle Hotel, St. Louis marital relations between us have not existed..

Have seen you only one day during the last four years and eleven months, that at a time in August 1927 when I went to Texas for that purpose.

I have been free to go to you at any time upon your request since June 1, 1928. Such request has not been received from you.

During the years mentioned you have contributed nothing toward my maintenance. Am now seeking through the Illinois Court a divorce.

I trust you will sign the self-explanatory papers which my representative and lawyer John M. Zane presents to you, so the same may be returned to this court for execution.

Your kindly well wisher, Susan.[8]

Letter from Susan to Charles
Dana Bice Collection

When Susan made the decision to divorce, she met with her cousin and attorney John Zane in Chicago. He prepared the necessary papers and traveled to Texas where Charles was then living. Zane returned to Illinois with Charles' signature and filed for divorce in the Circuit Court of Sangamon County. A divorce on the grounds of desertion and non-support was granted September 24, 1930, and 10 years after they had last been together as husband and wife, Susan and Charles were officially unmarried.[9]

Charles Gehrmann was found dead on May 20, 1944, in a room at the Silas Hotel in Springfield, two years before Susan's death. He was 81 years old. He had been residing in the hotel since the death of his sister in March of that year. He was survived by another sister in California, a brother in Kansas, and a cousin in Chicago.[10]

During the 10 years that Susan and Charles were estranged, Susan found a new sense of self, and she morphed into yet another identity. She discovered intellectual and leadership abilities that had not been tapped, and, for the first time, she led a full life without a man.

Notes on Chapter 13:

1. Susan Lawrence-Gehrmann to Marie Georgia, September 29, 1930, Box 1 ½, Folder 2, Dana Bice Collection.
2. Bill for Accounting #36017, Circuit Court Sangamon County, March 20, 1919.
3. Ibid.
4. Sangamon County Summons 65-10, March 22, 1919.
5. Plea in Abatement, of Charles A. L. Gehrmann, Circuit Court Sangamon County, May term, 1919.
6. Deposition of Charles Gehrmann, Oatman, Mohave County, Arizona, January 12, 1920.
7. Ibid.
8. Susan Lawrence-Gehrmann to Charles Gehrmann, Box 1 ½, Folder 2, Dana Bice Collection.
9. Divorce decree, Box 1 ½, Folder 2, Dana Bice Collection,
10. "Dr. C. A. Gehrmann claimed by death," *State Journal Register*, May 21, 1944, p. 10.

14

Susan Lawrence-Gehrmann: Political Activist

On February 15, 1923, Anita Pollitzer, National Secretary of the National Woman's Party (NWP), spoke at Susan's home to a non-partisan group of Springfield women. The speech was a call to arms for women to "unite to secure the same rights possessed by men under the law and remove the discriminations against women which still stand on the statute books of Illinois."[1] On February 18, the local newspaper read, "The National Woman's Party made public yesterday the announcement that Mrs. Susan Lawrence Gehrmann of Springfield had been appointed legislative chairman of the Illinois branch, National Woman's Party, and will take charge of the campaign to win legal equality for women with men, sponsored by its organization."[2]

Although Susan was a close friend with several public office holders, she had personally ventured into public service only on a few earlier occasions. In addition to the ill-fated work with the Illinois Commission Half-Century Anniversary of Negro Freedom in 1913, she was a member of the Executive Committee of the Sangamon County Republican women's organization in 1920.[3] In 1917 letters to Anna Lloyd Jones Wright, Frank Lloyd Wright's mother, she expressed her strong pacifist feelings about America's involvement in World War I.

> I am so wrought up over this dreadful war I can hardly settle myself to do anything. I am helping in every way that I possibly can, but it does not seem right for us to lend ourselves to wholesale murder. What good can possibly come to us in the sacrifice of the flower of the young manhood of the world? I can see none that will ever compensate for the loss.[4]

In a later letter Susan described her service on the home front:

> We were asked by the Council of Defense to put in a potato chip campaign so I took the chairmanship and sold over a thousand pounds at the state fair, on the streets, and at the theaters. We put them in 1½ ounce bags. [Laura Walker Brooks, a former maid in the Lawrence House, recalled that young girls sacked the chips in the house and then went out to sell them.[5]] I made for them over a thousand dollars, clear profit so feel repaid for all the work . . .We are busy every day doing Red Cross Canteen work. 65 days I fed 241 men—yesterday 64 men. We meet eight trains every day—I suppose we will keep the work up until all the soldiers have returned from Europe and sent to their destination.[6]

In 1923 history presented a political opportunity to Susan that appealed directly to her personal experience. Her marital ties with Charles virtually ended in May of 1920, and the Nineteenth Amendment granting women the right to vote was ratified in August of 1920. The extension of the voting franchise to women was just the beginning. The campaign for women's equal rights in all phases of life paralleled Susan's liberation from male dependence in her personal life. Susan felt the equal rights flame and became a primary torch bearer in Illinois.

After the announcement of her appointment as legislative chairman of the Illinois branch of the NWP, Susan immediately released a circular letter listing major inequities in Illinois law, several of which resonated soundly with Susan in her marital situation:

- The husband now is the only "head of the family." He may establish the legal residence of the family, and the wife legally has no choice.
- As in many states, the husband owns the wife's services. If a wife assists her husband in accumulating a fortune by her services in the home, or in his business, he is entitled to the whole of the fortune, because as her husband he is entitled to her services.
- In the case of personal injury to a married woman, two suits may be maintained, one by her for her pain and suffering and another by her husband for the loss of his wife's services. She has no corresponding right to his services and in case of injury to him, she can recover nothing.
- The father in Illinois may dispose of the custody of a minor child by will, except that he cannot deprive the mother of the custody of the children during her lifetime, without her consent. A mother can never appoint a guardian for her child unless there is no father.
- In Illinois women are ineligible for jury service, although they are serving on juries in 24 states.
- In granting letters of administration on the estate of a decedent, the father is preferred to the mother and the brother to the sister.[7]

The strategy was to pass brief "blanket" legislation to cover all of these inequities. Senator John Daily of Peoria, Illinois, introduced the bill which simply read:

Section 1. Be it enacted by the people of the State of Illinois represented in the General Assembly: Women shall have the same rights, privileges and immunities under the laws of this State as men.

Section 2. This Act shall be construed as abrogating in every respect the Common Law disabilities of women, and shall take preference over all other laws, and all laws and parts of laws which are inconsistent with this Act or any provisions hereof, are hereby repealed.[8]

Anita Pollitzer, Hatless in Center, With Unidentified Women
on Illinois State Capitol Steps May 17, 1923
Sangamon Valley Collection

Susan worked closely with the Washington D.C. based NWP, and she became close friends with several "stars" of the movement. Her strongest partner was the woman who recruited her, the party's young personable organizer and fund raiser Anita Pollitzer. Trained as an artist, Pollitzer was a friend of Georgia O'Keefe and O'Keefe's mentor/husband, Alfred Stieglitz. Earlier she had worked tirelessly for a woman's right to vote, and some credit her with getting the Nineteenth Amendment ratified. In August 1920, the night before a special session of the Tennessee legislature voted on the amendment, she dined with the 24 year old legislator Harry T. Burn. The next day, Burn changed his "no" vote to "yes" making Tennessee the 36th and decisive state to ratify the amendment.[9] Letters from Susan to Pollitzer were often signed "Mother Susan" or "Aunt Susie."

Two other officers of the NWP, Alice Paul, vice president, and Burnita Shelton Matthews, legal research secretary, frequently corresponded with Susan. Paul is remembered for her militant leadership in the suffrage movement. She organized large public rallies, parades, and protests and was imprisoned three times. After the ratification of the Nineteenth Amendment, she turned her energy and that of her organization toward winning equal rights for women.[10] Matthews was the young dynamic attorney who supervised the staff of the NWP Legal Research Department. They examined state codes for discriminatory laws and drafted legislation to eliminate gender bias. Additionally, Matthews, who would become the first woman appointed to the United States District Court, spoke eloquently on behalf of equal rights.[11] She traveled to Illinois on several occasions to promote the cause and was a guest in Susan's home.

Susan mounted a rigorous campaign starting with a rally at the Auditorium Hotel in Chicago with Senator Daily as featured speaker.[12] She buttonholed legislators and met with such diverse groups as the Chicago Social Agencies and the Amalgamated Garment Workers. She reported her work in her letters.

To Anita Pollitzer:

I have been planning and getting out all the printed matter, doing all the press work-- seeing these men--arranging for the hearing--informing Senator Daily all I can--presiding at a meeting in Chicago and two board meetings and for 10 days while in Chicago I had not more than three or four hours sleep out of 24.[13]

To Alice Paul:

I have circularized all Normal Schools and divisional Schools in the State, the Sangamon County Teachers Springfield area, and women employees in State House in number all, 1,563 persons. Sent a personal letter to each enclosed asking for support of bill.

Have gotten material into hands of every legislator's wife (204)--Every Woman's Party member (350) many times over. 4 times into hands of every legislator (204)=856 pieces in all.[14]

Earlier in a reading for Susan, astrologist Evangeline Adams had told her that ". . .all your life you will suffer more or less through your own sex because of one cause or another."[15] Unfortunately, that prediction proved true for Susan in the political arena. The largest obstacles to the passage of the legislation were the actions or inactions of women. Despite the fact that new members of the Illinois branch of the NWP were being recruited, Susan could not get others to help her. In a letter to Anita Pollitzer, she wrote:

I feel some times it is a hopeless task trying to legislate in the interests of women who refuse to even interest them enough to keep still, if they don't know what to say. Truly the inferiority complex has impinged more nerves and muscles than I had realized in the average woman. Psychoanalysis is not needed to detect it--it sticks out so plainly one can see little else, as they talk and chatter about being satisfied with things as they are.[16]

Illinois House Chamber, 1923
Sangamon Valley Collection

Furthermore, Lottie Holman O'Neill, the first woman to be elected to the Illinois House of Representatives, had introduced a bill which limited women's work day to eight hours. Daily's bill and the eight-hour law were pitted against each other. The eight-hour law was the kind of legislation supported by the social feminists who feared that the sweeping blanket legislation promoted by the NWP would undo and even prevent labor laws that protected women and promoted their welfare. A letter sent to Senator Daily and copied to all legislators from Julia C. Lathrop, State President of the League of Women Voters, explained the position that Susan was working against.

> While the Illinois League of Women Voters is working to secure for women legal rights not yet enjoyed by them in Illinois, we question whether this bill will accomplish that purpose. We also fear that some excellent legislation concerning women passed by men during the last fifty years may be endangered.
>
> The bill is indefinite in its wording and it is impossible to tell where it would strike...Is it wise or necessary to pass a law which would entail endless litigation?
>
> The phrase 'common law disabilities of women' no longer means anything in Illinois, for women, as such, have no 'disabilities' except possibly as to jury service. There are a few other discriminations against married women. These can be more definitely corrected by bills directed at the specific discrimination.[17]

Even the NWP staff seemed to undermine Susan's efforts. In letters to headquarters staff, Susan begged for national speakers to come to Illinois to challenge the League of Women Voters at various meetings. Refusing Susan's request, Anita Pollitzer responded in this way:

> . . .undoubtedly the opposition would like us to waste our strength and time at these meetings, the outcome of which they perfectly well know. Of course neither side has information enough as to the effects of blanket legislation on social laws to make anything we say more than an unprofitable debate.[18]

The final blow came from Mrs. Oliver Belmont, president of the NWP. Susan told the story in her own words:

> Up to the Eighth of May I had everything in my favor. I had enough votes in the House and Senate to pass our bill. Then gradually a turn came in the tide, a most subtle opposition began to make itself manifest and Senator Daily said to me several times he would give much to know what it meant. One day I had sent me by a friend in New York a copy of the *New York Times* containing an interview with Mrs. Belmont. It was entitled "Women to Set

Up a Rival Congress" stating we were to form a third national party entirely of women. Then I began to feel about and I discovered what was up--that had been used here. One man said, "Are you sure you are not representing a new political party?" I said why yes, then I showed him our declaration of principles and he said some one evidently has issued the double cross.[19]

Mrs. Belmont was a wealthy New York activist who had purchased the house just across the street from the nation's Capitol where the NWP was headquartered. In the May 1, 1923, edition of the *New York Times*, she made the startling announcement that she planned to form a third political party, a charge that Susan had repeatedly denied throughout the campaign. The house she had purchased was to be a place where women would come together into a parliament to debate the same subjects as Congress so the woman could "correct political evils."[20] This possibility alarmed the legislators, and the equal rights legislation was defeated as was the eight-hour law and all other laws that related to women's issues in that session.

Susan did not blame women entirely for the defeat. She wrote in one letter: "I am firmly convinced all men are liars."[21] This conclusion was undoubtedly drawn from both political and personal experience. She had been betrayed by both legislators and her estranged husband Charles. In another letter Susan noted that one legislator voted against the blanket bill because the women in his constituency "did not want it." Her response was: "It is good thing women's skirts are much more ample now--even a fat little man like him can hide behind them--however not very successfully. You know they are now often made of thin material and we can see through them."[22]

The Washington NWP staff was preparing for a major convention in Seneca Falls, New York, in July of 1923. Susan was encouraged to attend. She was also asked to be chairman of the Illinois branch of the NWP. She refused both. Totally exhausted from her efforts, she chose instead to recuperate at the cottage of Alice Henkle, another noted activist for women's rights, in Harbor Springs, Michigan.[23] Her future involvement in politics was minimal.

The NWP Seneca Falls convention of 1923 did not result in the formation of a third political party as Mrs. Belmont had envisioned. Rather Alice Paul introduced the Equal Rights Amendment (ERA), called the Lucretia Mott Amendment, which read: "Men and women shall have equal rights throughout the United States and every place subject to its jurisdiction." Anita Pollitzer seconded Alice's motion. This event initiated a national campaign in which the ERA was introduced in Congress every year after that until 1972 when it was finally passed. Mrs. Belmont's house became the Sewall-Belmont House and Museum on Capitol Hill which explores the evolving role of women and their contributions to society through educational programs, tours, exhibits, research and publications. The NWP still owns, maintains, and interprets the national historic landmark.

Susan's penchant to go against the grain of society was strongly tested in her single-handed battle for the equal rights legislation. She had found women like herself whose self-reliant individualism led them to action. Unfortunately, the sisterhood was not strong enough to achieve their goal in their lifetime.

Notes for Chapter 14:

1. "Emancipate girls; give women same status as men speaker urges," *Illinois State Register,* February 15, 1923, p. 2.

2. "Springfield woman will lead in fight for absolute equality of men and women under state laws" *Illinois State Register*, February 18, 1923, p. 10.

3. "To be County GOP women's lunch guest," *Illinois State Journal*, March 25, 1920, p. 11.

4. Susan Lawrence-Gehrmann to Anna Lloyd Jones Wright, July 29, 1917, Taliesin West Collection, #870496, Getty Research Institute.

5. Laura Walker Brooks, interviewed by Sella Morrison and Donald Hallmark, 1987, Dana-Thomas Collection.

6. Susan Lawrence-Gehrmann to Anna Lloyd Jones Wright, December 22, 1918, Taliesin West Collection, #870496, Getty Research Institute.

7. Susan Lawrence-Gehrmann to members of the National Woman's Party, February 17, 1923, National Woman's Party Papers.

8. Ibid.

9. Anonymous, "Anita Pollitzr (1894-1975) Officer and Organizer for Woman Suffrage" http://americancivilwar.com/women/Womens_Suffrage/Anita_Pollistzer.html.

10. Carol, Myers, and Lindman, "Alice Paul: Feminist, Suffragist, and Political Strategist" http://www.alicepaul.org/alicep3.htm.

11. Greene, Kate, "Burnita Shelton Matthews 1894-1988," in *Mississippi Women: Their Histories, Their Lives*, Elizabeth Anne Payne (Athens, Georgia:University of Georgia Press, 2003).

12. "Women launch fight on laws favoring men," *Chicago Tribune*, February 25, 1923, p. 2.

13. Susan Lawrence-Gehrmann to Alice Paul, March 8, 1923, National Woman's Party Papers.

14. Susan Lawrence-Gehrmann to Anita Politzer, April 2, 1923, National Woman's Party Papers.

15. E.S. Adams to Susan Lawrence Joergen-Dahl, November 4, 1912, Dana Bice Collection.

16. Susan Lawrence-Gehrmann to Anita Politzer April 14, 1923, National Woman's Party Papers.

17. Julia C. Lathrop to Illinois legislators, March 3, 1923, National Woman's Party Papers.

18. Anita Politzer to Susan Lawrence-Gehrmann March 20, 1923, National Woman's Party Papers.

19. Susan Lawrence-Gehrmann to Burnita Matthews, June 18, 1923, National Woman's Party Papers.

20. *New York Times,* May 1, 1923.

21. Susan Lawrence-Gehrmann to Burnita Matthews, June 18, 1923, National Woman's Party Papers.

22. Susan Lawrence-Gehrmann to Burnita Matthews, June 20, 1923, National Woman's Party Papers.

23. Susan Lawrence-Gehrmann to Anita Pollitzer, July 19, 1923, National Woman's Party Papers.

15

Susan Lawrence-Gehrmann: Seeker of Truth

While Susan had found guidance through the spirit letters from her parents and husbands, she did not limit herself to mediums for answers to her questions and for reassurance. For example, J.M. Fitzgerald completed a copy of a "Delineation of Character of Mr. L. Joergen-Dahl" in 1912.[1] Fitzgerald was a famous Chicago practitioner of phrenology, the study of the relationship between a person's character and the shape of his or her skull. He was a familiar name in Chicago because he was frequently called upon by court officials to analyze the character and personality of accused criminals. The analysis by Fitzgerald revealed that Lawrence was of upstanding character and therefore a good candidate for marriage.

Susan also consulted astrologists. Evangeline Adams of New York City, one of the most famous and successful astrologists of that time, gave Susan astrological readings. Adams established her place in history when she was arrested for fortune telling (an illegal practice in New York) and was acquitted after she gave an astrology reading for the judge's son. Several of her books and her autobiography vividly chronicled the astrology world in the early twentieth century.[2] The first surviving letter to Susan from Adams was in response to questions Susan posed while she was in Europe with Joergen-Dahl. The letter indicated that Susan had some misgivings about her new mother-in-law because Adams wrote: "I can see just why you have been worried on account of his mother, as the Moon, which stands for women, is the most afflicted planet in your chart."[3] The other surviving letter from Adams was dated after Joergen-Dahl's death, April 25, 1914. Susan had evidently inquired about future travel plans. Adams responded, "I think it would be all right for you to go abroad, but much better if you would go to some other part of the country and meet new conditions and people. You are under planetary conditions which might bring some very fine men into your life and they are always your friend."[4] Susan, of course, went to Oakland, California, shortly thereafter and married Charles Gehrmann.

While her marriage to Charles was disintegrating during the 1920s, Susan shifted from seeking answers and support from others to looking to her inner self through a movement called New Thought. New Thought is an umbrella term for diverse beliefs that emphasizes wholeness in mind, spirit, and body through constructive thinking, meditation, prayer, and the realization of the presence of God in everyone. Practitioners reject the dogma and doctrine of traditional religious organizations and emphasize the power of individual intuition.[5] The unconventional nature of New Thought appealed to Susan's independent spirit, and she assumed a new persona as a leader of the movement in Springfield.

Her involvement started in early February of 1921 when Dr. D. V. Bush, author of *Will Power: Your Possibilities,* gave a week-long series of free lectures on applied psychology and scientific living at the Springfield YWCA. Sponsored by the International Society of Applied Psychology, the talks included such topics as "How To Be Well, Happy and Prosperous" and "How To Love and Be Loved."[6] Following the public lecture series, Bush taught an advanced class in applied psychology which resulted in the creation of the Springfield Society of Applied Psychology, Mrs. Susan Lawrence-Gehrmann, president.

The newly-formed Society sponsored a series of 12 beginner's lectures and 12 advanced lectures by a Springfield New Thought leader, Frank Waller Allen, in September 1921. Allen had resigned from his position as pastor of Springfield's First Christian Church in 1917 to become a full-time journalist and lecturer on the principles of New Thought.[7] He wrote a column entitled "The Open Road" for the local newspaper and lectured at the Springfield College of Music and Allied Arts. Additionally, he lectured in several other states (often under the sponsorship of the International Association of Lions Clubs) and published essays in national publications.[8] He was the Springfield Society of Applied Psychology's primary teacher until he moved to Los Angeles where he taught at the Metaphysical Library, a New Thought institution.[9] Over the three years of its existence, the Springfield Society of Applied Psychology was very active, sponsoring several guest lecturers. It was the psychology class members who helped Susan send notices of meetings, bulletins, letters to legislators, and literature from the National Woman's Party (NWP) during her unsuccessful legislative campaign. When Allen left Springfield in December 1923, however, very few members remained in the organization.

When Susan had recovered from the failure of the equal rights legislation, she turned her energies back to exploration of religious thought. In May 1924, she established the Lawrence

Mary Meek
Unity Church Archives

Metaphysical Center in her home, and Mary Meeks, mother-in-law of Frank Waller Allen, became the instructor. Within a month, the name was changed to the Lawrence Center for Constructive Thought.[10] The center's studies went beyond applied psychology. Mary Meeks taught metaphysical classes, and special speakers discussed various phases of New Thought in the library and gallery of the Lawrence House. In addition to its regular programming, the center sponsored speakers of national reputation in venues other than the Lawrence House. The newspapers announced events at the center almost weekly.

The center offered classes for grade school children. One of those children recalled years later:

> We phoned ahead and were met at the garden gate by Mrs. Gehrmann and were taken to the library for classes. . .As the basis for our discussions, we used articles from *Wee Wisdom* magazine, published by Unity, Inc. Classes were kept small—only five or six. . .Classes were on Saturdays at 10 am and lasted an hour. . . Children's classes at Lawrence House went on for three years, at least (1923-1926).[11]

Unity literature was used in most classes at the center. Mrs. Meeks had been drawn to the Unity School of Christianity, one New Thought movement. Soon she resigned her position as teacher and principal in Decatur, Illinois, schools and became a licensed Unity teacher.

Susan explored other non-traditional philosophies and religions. She has been described as a "faithful attender" of the Theosophical Society, Springfield Branch, meetings. She traveled to Chicago in 1925 to attend the international convention of the Theosophical Society with members of the Springfield Branch.[12] The Lawrence Center was also a place where members of the local Baha'i movement met. The group was small and met in members' homes on Friday nights and at the Lawrence Center on special occasions. One member of that early group recalled that when Dr. Albert

"Moon Children"
by Richard Bock
Dana-Thomas House
Archives

Vail, a renowned Baha'i author and lecturer, came to Springfield, about 20 people sat on folding chairs around the "Moon Children" fountain for his lecture.[13] Baha'i records also indicate that Susan hosted dinners at her home for the group.

In October 1925, meetings of the Lawrence Center of Constructive Thought were moved to 231 Lawrence Street, the smaller house across Third Street. When Susan and Mrs. Meeks decided that more people would attend classes in a public place rather than a private home, the Lawrence Center moved in 1927 to the second floor of a building Susan owned at 225 South Sixth Street, and in 1929, the Lawrence Center became Lawrence Unity Center for Constructive Thought. The Center offered a circulating library and book shop service.[14] Many of those books could have come from Susan's extensive and eclectic private collection. The inventory of her books that were sold at the auction of her property in 1942 included works on oriental religions, psychic phenomena, astrology, theosophy, spiritualism, occultism, Swedenborgianism, Rosicrucianism, New Thought, Christian Science, reincarnation, numerology, Baha'i, and Gnosticism.[15]

Over the next several years, meetings of the Lawrence Unity Center were in two other downtown locations. By 1932 the organization dropped the Lawrence name and was called the Springfield Unity Center. It later became the Unity Society of Practical Christianity and then the Unity Church of Practical Christianity.[16] The congregation continues under that name at 417 East Cordelia Street in Springfield. Mary Meeks remained spiritual leader and teacher for 16 years. When she died, she was buried in the Lawrence family plot in Oak Ridge Cemetery.

For over three years the Lawrence House which Frank Lloyd Wright designed for social events was a center for seekers of spiritual answers. Prophetically, 20 years earlier Wright had commissioned Richard Bock to create a sculpture of a woman entitled "Flower in the Crannied Wall" to stand at the entry of the house. Alfred Lloyd Tennyson's poem by that same title is etched on her back. The poem proposes that all of the laws and meaning of existence in the universe can be found in a small flower and expressed the philosophy of Wright who once said, "I believe in God, only I spell it Nature." Tennyson wrote:

> Flower in the crannied wall,
> I pluck you out of the crannies—
> Hold you here, root and all, in my hand,
> Little flower—but if I could understand
> What you are, root and all, and all in all,
> I should know what God and man is.

Many in the Springfield community were welcomed by Bock's sculpture as they came to the Lawrence Center for Constructive Thought to "know what God and man is." As Frank Lloyd Wright had predicted, it was a "house to rest the soul."

"Flower in a Crannied Wall" by Richard Bock
Dana-Thomas House Archives

Notes for Chapter 15:

1. Joergen-Dahl folder, Box 11/2, Folder 4, Dana Bice Collection.
2. http://www.ofspirit.com/karenchristino1.htm.
3. Evangeline S. Adams to Susan Joergen-Dahl, November 4, 1912, Box 11/2, Folder 4. Dana Bice Collection.
4. Evangeline S. Adams to Susan Joergen-Dahl, April 25, 1914, Box 11/2, Folder 4, Dana Bice Collection.
5. http://www.beliefnet.com/Faiths/Christianity/New-Thought/Index.aspx.
6. "Bush will talk on applied psycholory," *Illinois State Journal,* January 26, 1921, p. 5.
7. http://www.unityofspringfield.com/frank%20allen.htm.
8. "Allen to give lecture series on psychology," *Illinois State Journal*, February 19, 1922, p. 22.
9. http://www.unityofspringfield.com/frank%20allen.htm.
10. Notice, *Illinois State Journal,* September 28, 1924, p. 12.
11. Lorraine (Fredrick) Tillden to Richard Taylor, May 7, 1985, Dana-Thomas Collection.
12. Ibid.
13. Aden Lochner, interviewed by Richard Taylor, 1985, transcript, SVC.
14. *Illinois State Journal,* November 7, 1926, p. 5.
15. Inventory, S. Lawrence, 20 August 1942, Inventory Record No. 27, Illinois Regional Archives Depository Center, University of Illinois Springfield.
16. http://www.unityofspringfield.com/Our%20History.htm

16

Susan: Friend

Although her marriages to men were ill-fated, many of Susan's friendships with women were long and fulfilling. The most notable were the friends she maintained from childhood. Leigh Gross Day was one of those friends. Leigh and Susan were in the same elementary class at the Bettie Stuart Institute. Leigh was an accomplished poet, artist, and photographer. She published several books in which she combined her skills by writing poems and illustrating them with photographs embellished with artistic flair. Many of the photos were taken in front of Susan's home or in her garden. Leigh Gross Day was also a contributor to several magazines including the *Ladies' Home Journal* and the *Woman's Home Companion.*[1] She was a member of the staff of the *Burr McIntosh Monthly*, a magazine published from April, 1903 to May, 1910, that featured photographs of celebrities of the day as well as landscapes, seascapes, children, and more. McIntosh, a New York publisher, offered a unique concept to his readers by binding the publication in string so that they could take it apart and display their favorite images.[2]

The largest party of the 1907 Springfield holiday season was not at the Lawrence House but at the Illini Country Club. An extravagant bridge party hosted by Leigh Gross Day celebrated Susan's return home from her six month trip abroad. The local newspaper reported that, "each of the 12 countries [visited by Susan] was represented at the party by a bridge table. The manner of finding the places was unique. Post cards from the country represented by the tables were used. The prizes were charming and original and the work of the hostess herself. They were calendars of watercolor designs containing the coat of arms and also a picture of Mrs. Dana taken by Mrs. Day."[3]

Susan (circa 1907) Photographed by
Leigh Gross Day
Dana-Thomas House Archives

Photos at the Lawrence House by Leigh Gross Day

All Photos from Dana-Thomas House Archives

Several other childhood friends remained in Susan's life well into her middle years. For example, Mary McRoberts Messerly was a neighbor of Susan when she was young. She was frequently among the guests or a co-hostess with Susan at many Springfield social events. In 1884 Mary married Charles Messerly, dry goods merchant and mayor in Sedalia, Missouri. Despite the fact that Mary firmly established herself in the society of Sedalia, the two women maintained a close friendship. Susan frequently traveled to Sedalia for extended visits, and Mary often returned to Springfield. Charles Messerly was a pall bearer at Joergen-Dahl's funeral.

Susan hosted an elaborate multi-day party for 11 out-of-town guests in November, 1921, a time when she had given up most entertaining. The guest list included Mrs. Charles S. Deneen of Chicago (wife of the 1905-1913 Illinois governor), Mrs. Alice T. Pillsbury of Pasadena, California (wife of the head of Pillsbury Mills Company whom Susan met 25 years earlier when she was living in Minneapolis), Mrs. George Halbert of New Orleans, Louisiana (Susan's cousin), and Mrs. Charles E. Messerly of Sedalia, Missouri.[4] Unlike the elaborate multi-day party she hosted in 1906, the 1921 gala guest list included only women. Notably they were all women she had known over long periods of time.

In addition to her loyalty, Susan was extremely generous with her friends. Young Susan Hoffman continued to be the recipient of Susan's generosity long after the Lawrence House grand opening. Mr. and Mrs. Hoffman and little Susan lived with Mr. Hoffman's parents in the caretaker's cottage just inside Oak Ridge Cemetery. (His father was the caretaker.) "Aunty Dana" often stopped at their home when she came to visit the graves of her family. Years later, young Susan told her daughter that "Aunty Dana" always wore a corsage of fresh flowers which she removed and gave to the child at each visit. "Aunty Dana" frequently suggested that little Susan come to stay with her. Susan Hoffman took her literally, and although she was in awe of "Aunty Dana," she feared her. One Easter "Aunty Dana" invited the child to her home for the holiday. Her mother Clara made a special dress for the occasion, and when the young Susan got dressed, she adamantly refused to go because she thought she would have to stay at the Lawrence House. Her parents finally relented and didn't force her to go. Instead they had a professional portrait made of Susan in her dress as a gift to "Aunty Dana."[5]

The close relationship between the families also extended to young Susan's father Fred. He had painted all the floors and walls in the Lawrence House. After the house was completed, he returned frequently to touch up spots that were damaged and to do other minor jobs. Susan's mother Mary also paid him to make repairs at the Lincoln Colored Home. Mary and Susan invited Fred for dinner frequently and asked his advice on many topics.[6] Fred told his granddaughter that he often took canned goods made by his wife to the Lawrence House, and Mary Lawrence was especially fond of homemade ketchup and sauerkraut. Fred Hoffman was one of the honorary pall bearers at the funeral of Mary Lawrence.[7]

Hanna Reilly, a widow who had moved to Springfield and built a home for herself and her son on North Ninth Street, frequently assisted Susan. She helped serve at parties and cared for the family pet parrot Polly when Susan traveled. When Hanna Reilly died, Susan brought a burial dress for her to her home.[8] Charlotte (Ide) Jess, a neighbor in her childhood, recalled that, "Anybody that had any sickness in the family or death she would be there to help out. She always provided an orchid for them to put in their hand in the casket."[9]

Susan's generosity and loyalty to her friends proved to be financially disastrous in at least one case. She became close friends with Frank Lloyd Wright's aunts, Nell and Jennie Lloyd (collectively called "the aunts"), when she lived in Minneapolis. In 1886 the aunts had established Hillside Home School, a progressive kindergarten through twelfth grade coeducational boarding school on the Lloyd property near Spring Green, Wisconsin. The school thrived, and in 1903 it was officially incorporated with six stockholders who were board members. Five of the six were Lloyd family members. Susan was the other stockholder.[10] By 1907 Hillside reportedly housed 100 students and teachers, most of them from Chicago. In late 1907 James Lloyd, brother of the aunts, was killed in a tragic accident. Unfortunately, he was badly in debt at the time of his death, and family members including the aunts had co-signed many of his notes. This presented a large financial setback, and for two years the aunts struggled to maintain the school. In September 1909 they declared bankruptcy. Another of their brothers, Jenkin (Jenk), came forward and bought the stock, and the school was once again running. New conflict arose when Jenk refused to return the stock to the aunts and proposed that the school become a state school.[11] Furthermore, scandals about the aunts' nephew, Frank Lloyd Wright, were emerging in the Chicago papers. Wright was building Taliesin, his dream home, on the property. The *Chicago Tribune* and the *Chicago Examiner* published stories of the still-married architect living there in his "love nest" with Mamah Borthwick Cheney, the wife of one of his clients.[12] Parents withdrew their students en mass. The combination of circumstances put the school once again in bankruptcy, and it closed for good in 1915.

Throughout this turmoil Susan remained on the board of Hillside and a friend with all the family members. Despite the fact that she felt that the aunts lacked good business sense, she gave many gifts and loans to them over the years. When the school closed, Frank Lloyd Wright bought it for $1 and assumed financial responsibility. At the time of the closing, Susan held a note with $2,000 principal and $1,400 interest due on it. Wright offered her a settlement that was considerably less and sent her some art prints presumably in payment. Susan was hurt and offended.[13] However, she continued to correspond with Wright and other family members for many years after Hillside closed.

Susan's generosity extended to her neighbors. She hosted a neighborhood tea party each Wednesday in her home.[14] She was especially kind to the neighborhood children. Gertrude (Bartel) Durkin who lived across the street from the Lawrence House recalled that after Gertrude's mother died, Susan brought the three-year-old Gertrude to her home and allowed her to run up and down the bowling alley. Gertrude also remembered that Susan would bring gifts from abroad for the five Bartel children including rosaries from Rome. Each of the five children received a rosary with the appropriate birthstone. The children were also invited to parties in the living room of the Lawrence House. They played games, ate snacks, and went home with favors Susan had bought on her travels.[15] Charlotte (Ide) Jess reported that at some parties for children, Susan had the plants in the long corridor that connects the entertainment area with the rest of the house replaced with water and gold fish.[16]

One group of children benefited from Susan's generosity in a unique way. John L. Lewis, president of the United Mine Workers of America and another Springfield native, called a national coal miners' strike in May 1919. Because violence was anticipated, Springfield schools were closed, but Susan invited one class to complete the term in her home. One of the members of the class reported that they met on her porch, and at the close of the term she gave an elaborate dinner party for the class and instructor.[17]

Susan's kindness and commitment to her friends is well illustrated by her relationship with Celia Hughes, a Chicago medium who became a very close friend and even traveled with Susan on one trip to Europe. In February 1909 a very ill Celia traveled from Chicago to the home of another friend, Jennie Willits, and her physician husband in Keithsburg, Illinois. Dr. Willits and Dr. Percy, another local physician, determined that Celia required surgery. Despite suggestions by Jennie Willits that Celia return to Chicago for the procedure, she chose not to do so. According to Jennie ". . .she said she would much rather not be there and then thought it might be so Doctor Willits could get her operation cheaper by being a friend of Dr. Percy. And she had paid out so much before in hospital and doctor bills she was discouraged."[18] Instead, the surgery was performed at a hospital in nearby

Galesburg, Illinois. Celia requested that a ring Susan had bought her in Europe be returned to Susan and that she be notified immediately if anything happened.[19] Celia did not survive the procedure. She died on March 10, 1909.

Susan's first action after her friend's death was to ask the undertaker to delay the embalming. According to a local newspaper, "Mrs. Hughes was a spiritualist medium and has often been in trances that resembled death and the delay was asked for fear that she might this time be in such a trance."[20] The undertaker complied with Susan's wishes for less than 24 hours. He then conducted tests which he documented in a letter to Susan and assured her that her friend was indeed dead.[21] Susan paid for the embalming, the casket, the cost of transporting the casket to Chicago, and the cremation by a Chicago undertaker. Susan also mediated the distribution of her deceased friend's worldly goods. The urn containing the ashes of Mrs. Hughes was found 35 years later in the Lawrence House when Susan's possessions were being inventoried for auction. It was buried in the family plot in Oak Ridge Cemetery.

Susan was often called upon to care for others in illness or after death. She wrote in the December 22, 1918, letter to Anna Lloyd Jones Wright:

> My cousin Miss Lawrence (she lives with me) was taken very sick last Christmas night, for five weeks I nursed her—I could get no help—we thought she could not possibly live and she gradually recovered [and] was up about the house for a month, then had a relapse and for six weeks I went over the same road night and day. . .June 1st my cousin in New Orleans Mrs. Hallert (you remember her) lost her husband very suddenly, I went there to help her settle up his affairs—was with her all the month of June, then brought her home with me— she stayed until October 1st. In July Mr. Dana's mother died. I went and helped care for her— afterwards I helped a friend with his mother—she passed out and we laid her away.[22]

In a letter to a friend Susan wrote:

> My two God children husband & wife with their young lady friends were struck in their auto by an interurban train--crushed them all badly killed my Goddaughter--28 years old the mother of the lively babies 1-3 & the other 18 months old. The father was all cut to pieces, is improving now. The young girls all had concussions of the brain but are improving. I had my hands full for weeks.[23]

Most of Springfield's citizens considered the woman who lived in the Lawrence House to be an anti-establishment eccentric. A few of them benefited by her largesse which she apparently extended to all who were fortunate enough to know her well. The examples of Mary and Rheuna that Susan observed in her early years were not forgotten in her own adulthood.

Notes for Chapter 16:

1. Elizabeth Butler, Interviewed by Richard Taylor, 1978, transcript IHPA archives.
2. *Guide to the Burr McIntosh Photograph Collection,* The New York Historical Society
   http://dlib.nyu.edu/eadapp/transform?source=nyhs/mcintosh.xml&style=nyhs/nyhs.xsl&part=body
3. "Lawrence center opens book service," *Illinois State Journal,* December 31, 1907, p. 12.
4. "Gehrmann party will be guests at many fetes," *Illinois State Journal*, November 17, 1921, p. 9.
5. Audrey Vieau, interview by author, May 24, 2010.
6. Susan Lorscheider, interview by Richard Taylor, 1981, transcript IHPA files.
7. Ibid.
8. Joan (Reilly) Smith, interviewed by author, July, 2010.
9. Gertrude (Ide) Jess, interviewed by Richard Taylor and Regina McGuire, 1984, transcript Dana-Thomas
   Collection.
10. "Articles of Organization" Hillside Home School, Wisconsin Historical Society.
11. Susan Lawrence-Dana to Nell and Jennie Lloyd, April 6, 1912, Lloyd Jones Collection.
12. Secrest, Meryle, *Frank Lloyd: a Biography* (New York:Alfred A. Knopf, 1992), p. 212.
13. Susan Lawrence-Gehrmann to Frank Lloyd Wright December 22, 1916, Taliesin West Collection,
   #L001C09, Getty Research Institute.
14. Anonymous, Dana-Thomas Collection.
15. Gertrude (Bartel) Durkin, interviewed by Richard Taylor, October, 1984, transcript Dana-Thomas
   Collection.
16. Gertrude (Ide)Jess, interviewed by Richard Taylor and Regina McGuire, 1984, transcript Dana-Thomas
   Collection.
17. Anonymous to Richard Taylor, undated.
18. Jennie Willets to Susan Lawrence Dana, March 18, 1909, Box 11/2, Folder 5, Dana Bice Collection.
19. Ibid.
20. "Embalming delayed," *The Republican Register,* March 10, 1909, p. 1.
21. Fred A. Dean to Susan Lawrence Dana March 12, 1909, Box 11/2, Folder 5, Dana Bice Collection.
22. Susan Lawrence-Gehrmann to Anna Lloyd Jones Wright, December 22, 1918, Taliesin West Collection,
   #870496, Getty Research Institute
23. Susan Lawrence-Gehrmann to Alice Pollitzer July 19, 1923, National Woman's Party Papers.

17

Susan Lawrence: Head of Household

Contrary to the custom and law of the day, both the 1910 and the 1920 U.S. census listed Susan, a woman, as the head of household at the Lawrence House. In that capacity she not only hosted legendary parties but also oversaw staffs of varying numbers, accommodated house guests for short and long stays, and personally carried out the many domestic duties needed to sustain such a large home. Through most of those years, two residents were always in the house—Cousin Flora and Polly, the parrot.

Although Cousin Flora, who was nine years Susan's senior, was a constant in Susan's life, little information survives about her. One of her obituaries notes that she was an avid reader.[1] Laura (Walker) Brooks who worked as a cook for Susan, called her "bossy" and recalled that Flora occasionally played the player organ that Frank Lloyd Wright had installed on the gallery overlooking the main reception area of the home.[2] After suffering for many years, Flora died on May 27, 1928, just two days before her 75th birthday. During her last years she suffered from myelitis, a neurologic syndrome caused by inflammation of the spinal cord. Susan described those years with her last remaining family member in a 1936 letter to Frank Lloyd Wright and his third wife Olgivanna:

> I never left her night or day during six and a half years. She had disintegration of the spinal cord—agonizing suffering and sometimes 20 bad convulsions in 24 hours. I was the only one who could control them. When she passed, I was left, as it were, a piece of human drift wood.[3]

Florence Lawrence
Dana-Thomas House Archives

More stories of Polly the parrot, evidently the only pet to live in the house, survive than accounts of Flora's life. Laura (Walker) Brooks recalled this incident:

Miss Flora and I was in the breakfast nook [the place where the parrot's cage was kept] and there was a fly in there. Miss Flora was hittin' at this fly but the parrot thought she was hittin' at me. . .and she like to tore up that cage to get her. The parrot thought she was hittin' me. Miss Flora would get so much kick out of that. Sometimes when she wanted a good laugh, she'd say, "Laura, come here," and I'd go there and she'd take my dress and fan me just to see that parrot act up.[4]

Polly was a chatterbox. Laura (Walker) Brooks sometimes thought Susan was calling her name only to discover that the parrot was summoning her.[5] Charlotte (Ide) Jess remembered that Polly would call, "Oh George" (one of Susan's staff) while perched on the porch.[6] Hannah Reilly recalled that when Susan traveled extensively, Mrs. Reilly would take the parrot into her home. The parrot wanted coffee and toast each morning. If the breakfast was not available when she was ready, Polly would perch on the top of the Reilly icebox and, using very salty language, demand to be fed.[7]

In addition to the permanent residents and the assorted guests and relatives who came and went through the house, Susan extended her passion for the arts by sheltering needy artists on at least two occasions. Laura (Walker) Brooks remembered Peter, a guitar player who was begging for food from house to house when Susan invited him to stay at her home. She hosted recitals by him with a free will collection and gave him the money. One day he announced to Laura that he was leaving because someone told him that Susan was making money off him. Laura and Susan could not convince him otherwise, and he left.[8] Her generous hospitality to artists was ill-fated again according to her cousin J. George Jefferson.

He wrote:

> Susie had an idea of turning the big house into an art museum and she let some young
> artists live in the carriage house. They turned out to be undesirables at the time and she had to
> have the police remove them.[9]

As her social life declined, the size of the staff that helped Susan maintain the house and entertain the guests shrunk. According to the 1910 U.S. Census, she had three African-American live-in staff members: Ada Bostick, cook; Bessie Nelson, maid; and Willis Hoskins, coachman.[10] Thomas and Mattie Walker, who were married after meeting at the Lawrence House, lived elsewhere. Mattie worked briefly as another cook, and Thomas served as night-time caretaker after he finished his day job as custodian at the First Presbyterian Church. He continued working at the house into the 1930s.[11] The only live-in staff listed in the 1920 census was George White, another African-American who was described in the census as a "wage worker working on own account rather than salary."[12] Laura Brooks, who worked for Susan in the late teens, remembered several other women who came in to clean, cook, and do laundry. Only Laura Brooks and George White, who tended the yard and the horses, lived on the premises.[13] By the 1930's when Susan had moved to the cottage, the only full-time staff was a caretaker/night watchman. Other staff was hired as needed.[14]

Susan maintained a close relationship with her staff, and they were loyal to her. Laura remembered that Susan invited her for dinner after Laura married and stopped working. Susan gave her a chest of silver for a wedding gift. When Russell Clem, one of her staff, was married, Susan had a celebration dinner for the couple. Another of her staff, Mary Moore, traveled to Germany with Susan.[15] Susan was especially close to George White whose body was viewed in the Lawrence House after his death.[16]

Thomas Walker
Dana-Thomas House Archives

Unidentified Maid
Dana-Thomas House Archives

In the late teens and early twenties, Susan assumed many domestic responsibilities herself. In her 1918 letter to Anna Lloyd Wright she referred to the fact that she had been housecleaning and cataloging her library.[17] She wrote to Burnita Matthews of the National Woman's Party (NWP) after the defeat of the Illinois Equal Rights Amendment, "I am very tired and find myself plunged into summer heat with all my business neglected for this legislative work. So now I must take up the grind of personal business—sewing, housecleaning, etc."[18] She sent a Christmas cookbook to friends in 1921 presumably with her own recipes. The contents ranged from meat (roasted fowl and ham) to desserts. The following "Pudding Sauce" recipe from her collection is particularly interesting for two reasons. Evidently cooks in 1921 did not worry about the dangers of serving uncooked eggs, and Susan was not concerned about Prohibition, the law of the land which was in effect from 1920 to 1933.

> 4 eggs (beaten separately) To each egg add ½ cup of granulated sugar while beating. Add to yolks after beating 3 tablespoons of whiskey (if you have it) as this helps to cook the eggs, otherwise flavor with lemon or vanilla. Add the whites to the yellows and beat. Then add 2 tablespoons of melted butter and serve immediately. Do not let it stand.[19]

Life at the Lawrence House was undoubtedly quite different from the images implied by the press and gossip. As the years went on, Susan's fortunes diminished and her interests shifted. The butterfly of the early years became faded and, at times, resembled a worker bee.

Notes for Chapter 17:

1. "Miss Lawrence, 75, dies after long illness," *Illinois State Journal*, May 28, 1928, p. 2.
2. Laura (Walker) Brooks, interviewed by Sella Morrison and Donald Hallmark, 1987, Dana-Thomas Collection.
3. Susan Z. Lawrence to Olgivanna and Frank Lloyd Wright December 4, 1936, Taliesin West Collection, #L038D04, Getty Research Institute.
4. Laura (Walker) Brooks, interviewed by Sella Morrison and Donald Hallmark, 1987, Dana-Thomas Collection.
5. Ibid.
6. Gertrude (Ide) Jess, interviewed by Richard Taylor and Regina McGuire, 1984, Dana-Thomas Collection.
7. Joan (Reilly) Smith interview by author, 2010.
8. Laura (Walker) Brooks, interviewed by Sella Morrison and Donald Hallmark, 1987, Dana-Thomas Collection.
9. J. George Jefferson to Dick Taylor, July 13, 1935, Dana-Thomas Collection.
10. U.S. Census of the United States: 1910-Population.
11. Alelia (Walker) Clem, interviewed by Donald Hallmark, 1982, IHPA archives.
12. U.S. Census of the United States: 1920-Population.
13. Laura (Walker) Brooks, interviewed by Sella Morrison and Donald Hallmark, 1987, Dana-Thomas Collection.
14. Alelia (Walker) Clem, interviewed by Donald Hallmark, 1982, IHPA archives.
15. Ibid.
16. Laura (Walker) Brooks, interviewed by Sella Morrison and Donald Hallmark, 1987, Dana-Thomas Collection.
17. Susan Lawrence-Gehrmann to Anna Lloyd Jones Wright, December 22, 1918, Taliesin West Collection, #870496, Getty Research Institute.
18. Susan Lawrence-Gehrmann to Burnita Matthews, June 18, 1923, National Woman's Party Papers.
19. "Greetings from the Lawrence House" December 25, 1921 Dana-Thomas archives.

18

Susan Z. Lawrence (Aunt Susie): Declining Legend

On a cold winter night in 1927, Mrs. McDonald was serving dinner in her home across East Lawrence Street from Susan's small frame house. A single parent, "Mom" McDonald had a few boarders but supported herself primarily by serving lunch and dinner daily to paying guests. The group at the dinner table that evening included the regulars—Mr. and Mrs. Larsen and Clarence Klassen, all employees of the State Department of Health, Susan, and a newcomer who had moved to Springfield from Peoria recently. The stranger received a phone call during dinner, and when he returned to the table, he explained with tears in his eyes that his wife had a heart attack and died in Peoria. He told the group that he would have to wait until morning to return to his home because there were no more trains going in that direction that night. Susan, who had a cab driver who came when she wanted to go somewhere, went to the phone and ordered the best cab with a good heater. The cab picked up the bereaved man and took him to Peoria that night—at Susan's expense.[1]

Despite the fact that Susan was deeply in debt at that time, her compassionate generosity had not diminished. Her extravagant spending habits were undoubtedly a strong contributing factor to her crisis, but she herself cited several other causes for her financial condition in a 1931 letter she wrote to Georgia Jefferson, a cousin who was asking for a small loan. By Susan's own estimate, Flora's long illness cost her $25,000. She wrote:

> [I paid for] trained nurses night and day for over five years. . .opiates by the pounds, and doctor prescriptions for every few tablets and ounce of the liquid...Then this slump in the stock market [1929] caught everyone—even those who thought they were most secure in old tried and tested securities. . .I have lost $52,000 in rents in the last five years. My large store building on 6th has never been rented in all that time. . .In the next three months I have to pay over $3,000 interest and in April $5,700 taxes, and these unrented things will not yield the money to do it.[2]

Susan tried several strategies to recover her loses. She reluctantly mortgaged her two buildings in downtown Springfield to the Marine Bank. The bank assumed management and control of the properties and gave a $400 a month allowance to Susan. She could not repay the loan, and the debt kept mounting. Once again seeking answers from a non-traditional source, she turned to numerology, a metaphysical science whose practitioners study numbers in an individual's life and determine how those numbers relate to the spiritual, emotional, and physical well-being of that person. Susan consulted a famous New York numerologist, Ariel Yvon Taylor-Warren, who encouraged Susan's divorce from Charles Gehrmann and gave her advice on business matters.[3] Taylor-Warren wrote several books on numerology some of which have been re-printed several times and are available today. On her advice, Susan returned to her maiden name and added "Z" as a middle initial after her divorce.[4]

Susan was forced to make some lifestyle changes, and sometime in the late 1920s she moved from the Lawrence House to the small frame house that had served as the Lawrence Center for Constructive Thought across the Third Street tracks at 231 East Lawrence. She maintained a caretaker and occasionally had a woman come in to help her. Although the automobile had become the preferred mode of transportation, Susan never owned a car. She no longer had horses, but she kept her three carriages in the carriage house and depended on her favorite cab driver for transportation. She ate most of her meals at Mrs. McDonald's home.

Other regular diners at "Mom" McDonald's table recalled that at this point in her life, "Aunt Susie," as she was called then, continued to travel and would return with stories and recipes. They were not sure which of the stories to believe, but they enjoyed the dishes prepared from the recipes. "Aunt Susie" claimed that if she liked a dish she ate in a fine hotel, she would go into the kitchen and demand the recipe from the chef. Mrs. McDonald would make the dishes using gourmet ingredients that "Aunt Susie" bought in St. Louis where she went by cab. One Christmas "Mom" McDonald cooked the dinner in her kitchen with some help from "Aunt Susie," and the small group of Mrs. McDonald's diners ate in the dining room in the Lawrence House.[5]

Susan experienced several other misfortunes during the mid-1930s. She described a serious physical and emotional breakdown in a December 4, 1936, letter to Frank Lloyd Wright and his wife Olgivanna: "I found it necessary to resort to a complete rest cure—with the strict diet and every kind of treatment known to modern scientific methods. So I just buried myself and systematically have worked out my salvation—am getting better—and have retained the brain power and balance— at a very dear cost."[6] One of those costs was her home. She continued her letter to Olgivanna and Frank Lloyd Wright:

> My house here has been on the list of things I have not been able to look after and keep in constant repair. I could not take the necessary steps to look after it. I have always had a caretaker in it and have been in the small house on the other side of the railroad when I have been able to stay here.
>
> —have rolled the rug, packed away the draperies and furniture, cushions, etc. I have kept fire enough in the library to care for the books, but the furnace has proven inadequate for needs. Many pipes are out of condition. The four back rooms are connected with the city heat still so my caretaker can stay in the house.

To add to her problems, she was a victim of vandalism.

Lately I have been having trouble with boys stealing the copper downspouts off of the house. Only last week one morning at 5:30 am three boys—aged 12, 14, 17 years-- stole four inside the yard. My caretaker found the theft in half an hour. I had the detectives here in 15 minutes later, and in three hours we had the three boys and the father who sold 33 lbs. of the lovely copper downspouts to a junk dealer for $1.70. They had them pounded up. All were in the jail evidence & all with complete confession. Now they have been committed and are serving terms.

Finally, she told the Wrights that her property was disintegrating.

One morning the caretaker at 6:30 came across to me commenting that something dreadful had happened over there. 85 feet of the north garden wall—from the north gate post to the high peer at the garage --had gone over in to my neighbor's yard. Only the cement face was intact with one layer of brick attached. The square post at gate has been showing some slight signs for a long time of disintegration due to the vases having no drain connected with them down through the masonry in the posts. Now that this has happened we see inside the faulty construction and lack of insight in their erection. The water standing in the vases gradually seeping through has caused the disintegration. I am at a stand still. I do not know what to do. It would, from estimates, cost about 15 hundred to 2 thousand dollars to replace it—all.

This week the lot just north of us (house has been removed six months to avoid paying taxes on it) has been ½ sold to put up an apartment on it. I am hoping to find out more about this in a day or two—as to the plans for it and will have to do something about the fallen wall.[7]

In a note to Wright dated just three days later, Susan informed him that she had fallen. She wrote, "I split my head open—was unconscious for over an hour—then was taken to the hospital and had it stitched up." She desperately ended the barely decipherable note with "The line between my property and that on the north has come into question. They want to begin excavating immediately—I don't know what to do about it."[8] Frank Lloyd Wright responded to Susan's desperation by assuring her that he and Olgivanna would come to see her soon and "talk over" the fallen wall and the lot line.[9]

Excerpt of Note from Susan to Frank Lloyd Wright
Getty Research Institute

93

Unfortunately, the trip did not materialize as Wright planned. Two days after he wrote his assuring letter, Olgivanna sent a brief note to Susan. It was addressed to "My Dear Mrs. Lawrence" and signed "Mrs. Frank Lloyd Wright." She explained that her husband was in bed with a cold and unable to travel. They sent their good wishes.[10]

Finally, sometime in the spring of 1937, Mr. and Mrs. Wright and their daughter Svetlana drove from Spring Green, Wisconsin, and visited the house he had designed over 30 years before. Since the house continued to deteriorate, not all of the issues were resolved, but the effort made by the man whom Susan considered a friend undoubtedly served to boost her spirits.

A year later, December 10, 1937, Susan sent a night letter to Frank Lloyd Wright which read:

> Fell Sunday night top to bottom hard wood stairs small house cut long gash back of head was on floor unconscious 2½ hours then summoned doctor hospital many stitches taken returned here terrible loss of blood very weak close call badly bruised all over critical condition.[11]

Then on April 21, 1939, Susan wrote a note to Eugene Masselink, Mr. Wright's private secretary, explaining that she was trying to get in touch with Wright (who was en route to England) to discuss the possibility of selling her house to a fraternal organization. She was again incapacitated because a taxi in which she was riding was hit by a large truck from the rear. As a result, Susan had spine, neck, and head injuries as well as a dislocated right shoulder.[12] The response from Masselink was solicitous and polite. However, he informed her that he did not forward her letter "because there is hardly time for them to do anything before they are back here at Taliesin."[13] The relationship had obviously cooled.

Susan's friends and family were dying or abandoning her, she was losing her money, her home was deteriorating, and her body was failing her. To meet the many adversities that she faced, Susan was forced into drastic lifestyle changes. Unfortunately, even more indignities were in store for her.

*Mr. and Mrs. Wright at
the Lawrence House, 1937*
Dana-Thomas House Archives

Notes for Chapter 18:

1. Clarence Klassen, interviewed by Richard Taylor and Regina McGuire, 1985, Dana-Thomas Collection.
2. Susan Lawrence to Georgia Jefferson, January 22, 1933, Dana-Thomas Collection.
3. Yvon Taylor-Warren to Miss Susan H. Lawrence, Sept. 19, 1930, Box 1 ½, Folder 2, Dana Bice Collection.
4. Ibid.
5. Clarence Klassen, interviewed by Richard Taylor and Regina McGuire, 1985, Dana-Thomas Collection.
6. Susan Z. Lawrence to Olgivanna and Frank Lloyd Wright December 4, 1936, Taliesin West Collection, #L038D04, Getty Research Institute.
7. Ibid.
8. Susan Z. Lawrence to Frank Lloyd Wright December 7, 1936, Taliesin West Collection, #L037B08, Getty Research Institute.
9. Frank Lloyd Wright to Susan Lawrence December 10, 1936, Taliesin West Collection, #L037B10, Getty Research Institute.
10. Mrs. Frank Lloyd Wright to Susan Z. Lawrence December 12, 1936, Taliesin West Collection, #L038B04, Getty Research Institute.
11. Susan Z. Lawrence to Frank Lloyd Wright December 10, 1937, Taliesin West Collection, #L037B10, Getty Research Institute.
12. Susan Z. Lawrence to Eugene Masselink, April 21, 1939, Taliesin West Collection, #L046D01, Getty Research Institute.
13. Eugene Masselink to Susan Z. Lawrence, April 27, 1939, Taliesin West Collection, #L046D05, Getty Research Institute.

19

Susan Z. Lawrence: Invalid

The downward spiral continued as Susan began to exhibit eccentric behavior. Alelia Clem, a woman who was hired on the rare times when Susan had guests, remembered that there were many bundles of dish towels and boxes and unopened boxes of chocolates from a local candy manufacturer throughout the house.[1] One frequently repeated story was that the neighbors called the police when Susan and her cab driver friend celebrated one New Year's Eve by shooting a gun in the street outside her house.

On May 8, 1942, Susan's physician, Dr. Alex J. Jones, sent nurse Lucille Ramshaw to Susan's home to take her to the hospital. Lucille found Susan refusing to move from a filthy bed in a filthy house. Her cousins, Farnett Maxcy Radcliffe of Chicago and Margaret Maxcy Woodhall of St. Paul, Minnesota, were with her. Finally Lucille convinced Susan to go to St. John's Hospital to see Dr. Jones, and she called an ambulance from a local funeral home. When the attendants carried Susan from the bed on a liter, Lucille found a knife, gun, and five empty purses under her pillow. Lucille recalled that Susan was very dirty and almost dead from malnutrition when she got to the hospital.[2]

Four days later an incompetency hearing was convened in Sangamon County's probate court. Dr. Jones testified that Susan was no longer capable of attending to her own affairs because she had developed "senile psychosis." Her cousins supported his testimony by describing her disorientation and physical incapability. Refusing to eat or to be bathed, Susan was so verbally abusive to the nurses hired to care for her that they all quit. Susan Z. Lawrence was declared incompetent. At the request of Dr. Jones, his friend Earl Bice, a Springfield attorney who had never met Susan, was appointed conservator of her estate, and Farnett Maxcy Radcliffe was named conservator of her person.[3]

Earl Bice hired private nurses 24 hours a day seven days a week. Lucille Ramshaw became Susan's private day nurse for the first few years that she was at St. John's Hospital. She reported that Susan was content once she gained her strength. She described Susan as gracious, charming, regal, and never angry. Susan talked frequently about her father and her life with Joergen-Dahl as well as her travel adventures. She had her lucid times and her bizarre moments. Lucille recalled that Susan always said she was going to write a memoir of her father and demanded the daily paper so that she could write notes in the margins for her book. She then stashed the papers in drawers unread. Susan claimed that she had learned to belly dance from Little Egypt (Stage name for Frida Mazar Spyropoulos who introduced America to the dance at the 1893 and 1933 World's Fairs in Chicago). To prove her claim, she demonstrated the "hootchy-kootchy" to embarrassed young doctors and red-faced nuns.[4]

Bice, who provided money for Lucille Ramshaw to buy robes and gowns for Susan, visited her weekly, and Farnett Radcliffe came for a few days several times a year. The only other regular visitor according to Lucille was Mrs. Vincent Dallman, a long-time friend.[5] Others from Susan's past who remember visiting Susan included Laura Walker Brooks, one of her cooks, who recalled, "I went to the hospital to see her, and at the time they weren't letting nobody in, but she asked 'em who was out there, and the nurse said, 'a colored girl.' She said, 'Well, let her in.' So I got in to see her."[6] Susan (Sue) Lawrence Lorsheider, Susan's namesake, also visited her generous "Aunty Dana" at the hospital. She remembered that the elder Susan was "an ill woman of 80, a little senile, maybe, but not crazy like everyone said." Susan showed the younger Susan the cotton dresses that were hanging in her closet and said, "Look what they've reduced me to. Can you imagine me wearing this?" When "Aunty Dana" also expressed regret that she didn't have any pictures of herself, Sue Lorsheider brought her a photograph. When the younger Susan went to retrieve the picture, a nurse would not let her into the room and just handed her a folder with the photo signed in bright turquoise ink, "To Susan, From the Other Susan, 8-18-43."[7]

Lucille Ramshaw summed up those early hospital days in this way: "She looked forward to her meals and to being washed and pampered and petted—she loved it." In her senile state, ". . .there was nothing wrong with Susie. She could have been anyplace, but they allowed her to stay in the hospital. . .now she would be in a nursing home."[8]

Earl Bice's first project after he was named conservator was to inventory Susan's personal property. To complete the daunting task of listing all of the contents of the Lawrence House, Bice paid Irene Garvey and Eva Barber $125 to assist him and his wife Grace.[9] They found a lifetime collection which took weeks to catalog. The 35 page inventory reflected the many aspects of Susan's life. She was an art lover (Japanese prints, Satsuma wine pot [year 1640], marble statuettes), a world traveler (candle holder from Martinique, one of five hand-carved Dali Lamas from Tibet, Chinese incense burners), a fashion plate (81 fans, approximately 2,000 yards of fabric still on bolts, 109 scarves), a hostess (167 piece Dresden dinner service, one complete service for 20 of hand painted English dinnerware, 41 etched goblets), a housewife (257 baking dishes, three electric irons, electric sweeper), and a tragic victim (assorted baby clothes).[10]

One of Susan's major life roles, student of religious philosophy, was reflected in her library. In addition to her books on all kinds of religion, her collection of over 2,200 volumes included children's books, many classics, history books, woman's studies, and 250 travel books. Many of these were first editions. Like several other things in the house, some books were still in boxes, so it is not clear whether Susan was a reader, collector, or both. The Bice team also found a large collection of foreign coins and currency, multiple trunks of linens, assorted furniture, valuable rugs, and oddities such as a tom-tom and a campaign picture of Alfred Landon.

Susan's jewelry collection was extensive. Among the many expensive pieces was a necklace with 70 matching diamonds which Susan reportedly bought at Tiffany's and wore when she was presented at the Court of St. James and her mourning pin with her father's profile surrounded by 35 diamonds.[11] Conspicuously missing from the inventory were Susan's clothes. Years later Grace Bice recalled that a Chicago cousin, presumably Farnett Radcliffe, said that she did not want Susan's clothes to be sold. She wanted them destroyed. Mrs. Bice assumed that Susan's elegant gowns were burned.[12]

When the Bices completed the inventory, they took a train trip to all the cities and towns where Susan said she had lock boxes. Their stops included Chicago, San Francisco, Los Angeles, Salt Lake City, Leadville, Colorado, and Grants Pass, Oregon. At each bank they found only jars of parrot feathers in the lock box. They flew back to Illinois from Seattle, Washington, empty-handed.[13] Bice's final conclusion was that Susan's personal property was worth $57,386.11.[14]

One year after Susan was declared incompetent, Bice sought permission from the court to sell Susan's real and personal property. The two remaining mines in Colorado and Oregon were virtually worthless, and her Illinois real estate property was valued at $177,565.00. This included the building at the southeast corner of Adams and Sixth Streets (the Roland building), the building at 225-227 South Sixth Street, a vacant lot on East Brown Street, the Lincoln Colored Home (which had reverted to Susan because it was no longer being used for its original purpose), 80 acres of timberland in Logan County, the cottage at 231 East Lawrence Street, and the Lawrence House. In his report submitted to Bice, appraiser John Brinkerhoff evaluated the deteriorating Wright designed house in this way:

. . .a brick dwelling. . .which cannot be classed as a desirable piece of residential property. . .the arrangement and floor plan of the interior and the exterior appearance makes this house practically worthless for living quarters. My opinion is that unless this house could be sold to an organization. . .the only value it would have would be the wrecked value. It might be possible to sell this house and ground to [an organization] at a price bordering on $20,000... There is a great deal of very fine material in this house which would make it have a good sale price to a wrecking contractor, and I feel that for this purpose the house and ground would have a value of $13,175. . .The ground is a very good piece and under ordinary conditions I think would sell readily as it is a large piece and could be used for an apartment building, and should have a value of $8,175.00.[15]

Probate Court Judge Benjamin DeBoice chose the $20,000 figure as a price for the house and accepted Brinkerhoff's estimate of the fair value of the cottage and lot on Lawrence Street as $3,682.[16] Bice further testified that the $400 allowance from Marine Bank did not cover Susan's current hospital expenses. Lucille Flynn, a nurse who tended Susan in her later years, testified that she had become totally incompetent, could not feed herself, and was completely disoriented. On June 17, 1943, DeBoice authorized Bice to sell all real and personal property.[17]

Meanwhile, Bice had discussed the possibility of purchasing the entire estate with Morton D. Barker, one of the partners of the Barker, Goldman and Lubin Lumber Company. Barker agreed, and in July 1943 the Marine Bank of Springfield purchased the estate for $278,000 on his behalf. Since there was a debt of $164,473 of back interest on the mortgage on the Sixth Street properties and one of $13,000 on the Lawrence House, approximately $100,000 remained for Susan's care.[18]

The name of the buyer remained unknown to the public, and the Marine Bank served as the trustee of the estate. Barker had made the purchase primarily to acquire the two downtown South Sixth Street properties. Consequently, Susan's personal property and the cottage on East Lawrence were offered to the public in a six-day auction the week of July 26, 1943. The scope of the items for sale and the lore that surrounded Susan and her house aroused the community's curiosity, and after having a low profile for several years, Susan was back in the newspapers. Details of the sale were found in every paper every day for weeks. The vacant lot at Fourth and Cook Streets, the north end of the block from the Lawrence House, was fenced in. A large tent which could seat 1,500 on wooden folding chairs was embellished with bright lights and red decorations, and "once magnificent dress materials—satins and gold lames, by then moth eaten and decayed, were used to drape the 30 by 40 foot auction block."[19] A public address system was installed, and young boys walked through the crowd with buckets of iced drinks for the patrons.

Auction Ad
Dana-Thomas House Archives

Auction Tent, Fourth and Cook Streets
Abraham Lincoln Presidential Library & Museum

Plans to charge one dollar admission were abandoned after the first day when many Springfield citizens stood outside the tent and listened. The cottage at 231 East Lawrence was the first to be offered by Luke Gaule, chief auctioneer. It was bought by Chicagoan Morton A. Barker, cousin of the Springfield Morton D. Barker, for $3,175. Among other things, the unused baby clothes Susan purchased on her honeymoon with her second husband sold the second day. The layette had been on display in a local department store window for weeks preceding the auction.

The dramatic highpoint of the auction came on the fifth day when a Brinks armored car with seven plain clothed detectives carrying machine guns delivered Susan's jewelry which had been exhibited in another local store window. Her famed Tiffany-designed diamond necklace was appraised at $18,000 but sold for $7,000. Local jeweler Frank Bridge, the buyer, later broke up the necklace and Susan's mourning pin of her father to make individual diamond rings. When the bidding was complete, the armed guards returned the jewelry to the First National Bank vault where buyers picked them up the next day.

On the last night of the sale, the 1,200 patrons were reminded that the country was in the midst of World War II when Springfield was plunged into darkness for a practice air raid blackout. Coroner W. L. Dragoo added a festive touch by leading the crowd in song. When the lights returned a half hour later, the bidding continued. Among the items that were sold that night were Susan's two surreys and her one-of-a-kind replica of Teddy Roosevelt's carriage.

The sale was promoted nationally, and buyers and collectors came from throughout the country. The general public did not get the opportunity to bid on everything that was advertised. For example, the library of books went by a moving van to Brentano's, a Chicago bookstore. The "specially constructed furniture" (Wright's designs) was not sold because a prospective buyer of the house requested that the furniture remain with the building while he considered the purchase.[20]

Mercifully, Susan was not reading newspapers during the auction, so she was not aware of the event. The woman who had built a mansion, entertained lavishly, traveled the world, befriended many, championed the rights of women and African-Americans, shared her time and money, and led seekers of spiritual truths died February 21, 1946, at the age of 83 surrounded by strangers who were being paid to care for her. Wearing the dress she had chosen, Susan was buried in Oak Ridge Cemetery between her father and her first husband Edwin Dana. Her final estate included a seal fur coat with a mink collar, a table radio, an electric fan, a small Christmas tree with electric bubble lights (a gift from Bice), $25,000 in U.S. Treasury bonds, and $35,000 in U.S. Savings bonds. Susan's neighbor, Mrs. Eva McDonald, claimed $150 from the estate for personal services and meals from 1941 to 1942, but she was denied. After expenses, each of eight surviving first cousins inherited $6,154.25.

This brief paragraph in her obituary attempted to summarize Susan's life:

> Mrs. Lawrence lived a full and colorful life and her name was news not only in Springfield but beyond the borders of the state. With ample wealth at her command and possessed of unusual beauty, a gracious personality and strong loyalties, she was a leader in Springfield social circles for many years and was welcome in national and international society.[21]

However, the description only hinted at the enigma that was Susan who had re-invented herself at every twist and turn in her long life journey.

Lawrence Family Monument, Oak Ridge Cemetery

\

Notes for Chapter 19:

1. Alelia (Walker) Clem, interviewed by Don Hallmark, 1982, IHPA archives.
2. Lucille Ramshaw, interviewed by Richard Taylor, 1985, IHPA archives.
3. Incompetency Hearing, May 12, 1942, Incompetency File #5908, Sangamon County Circuit Clerk's Office, Springfield.
4. Lucille Ramshaw, interviewed by Richard Taylor, 1985, IHPA archives.
5. Ibid.
6. Laura Walker Brooks, interviewed by Sella Morrison and Don Hallmark, Dana-Thomas Collection.
7. Harty, Rosalynne "The Other Susan" *State Journal-Register*, September 20, 1981, p. 17.
8. Lucille Ramshaw, interviewed by Richard Taylor, 1985, IHPA archives.
9. Earl Bice to Miss Irene Garvey and Mrs. B. L. Barber, Box 36, Garvey Collection, Sangamon Valley Collection, Lincoln Public Library.
10. Appraisal Inventory, Susan Z. Lawrence, Incompetency File #5908, Probate Court of Sangamon County, Illinois.
11. Ibid.
12. Grace Bice, interviewed by Cecile Meiers, 1990, Dana-Thomas archives.
13. Ibid.
14. Appraisal Inventory, Susan Z. Lawrence, Incompetency File #5908, Probate Court of Sangamon County, Illinois.
15. John Brinkerhoff to Earl Bice filed June 14, 1943, Sangamon County Clerk of Probate.
16. Ibid.
17. Probate Court records, April 9, 1943.
18. "Lawrence estate sold to Marine Bank," *Illinois State Journal*, July 9, 1943.
19. Allen, Wayne and Meyer, Mary, "A Woman's Castle," *Illinois State Register*, January 6, 1956, p. 7.
20. "Auction sale not all fun," *Illinois State Register*, July 31, 1943, p. 1.
21. "Susan Z. Lawrence, scion of famed family, passes on," *Illinois State Register*, February 21, 1946, p. 1.

AFTERWORD

Susan's name reappeared in the Springfield newspapers occasionally in the decades to follow. In 1956 reporters Mary Myer and Wayne Allen wrote a four-part series entitled "A Woman's Castle: The Story of the Legendary Susan Lawrence Home" for Springfield's *Illinois State Journal-Register*. In November 1965 the *Journal-Register* published a three part series by Joan Muraro. Reporter Rosalynne Harty told Susan (Hoffmann) Lorschieder's story in the September 20, 1981 *Journal-Register*. Like the news stories written during Susan's lifetime, these features were a mixture of fact and myth, yet they illustrate the continuing fascination with Susan Lawrence.

The lavish house that Frank Lloyd Wright designed for Susan was sold to C.C. Thomas after the 1944 auction. Thomas was an admirer of Wright and converted the home into corporate headquarters for the Thomas Publishing Company while maintaining the integrity of the Wright design and preserving the furnishings and art glass. In 1981 the state of Illinois purchased from the Thomas family what was then called the Dana-Thomas House for one million dollars. The state closed the house in 1987 for a five-million-dollar restoration project to return the building to its 1910 condition, and in 1990 the state of Illinois opened the house to the public for tours. Thousands of people have since toured the over one hundred year old Wright masterpiece. It still looks very much like it did when Susan communicated with the departed, entertained Springfield's society, explored religious philosophies, and said goodbye to her loved ones.

ABOUT THE AUTHOR

Roberta Volkmann is an arts educator and freelance writer living in Springfield, Illinois. She trained as an interpreter of the Dana-Thomas House shortly after the State bought the house and has volunteered there since that time. Over the years Roberta served in many capacities on the Dana-Thomas House Foundation Board including president for two terms. She is the editor of the Dana-Thomas House education resources that are found at http://www.illinoishistory.gov/hs/dth.htm. Her other published works include travel stories featuring the arts, book reviews for *Music Educator's Journal*, and teacher's guides. She has co-authored with her husband Carl *Springfield's Sculptures, Monuments, and Plaques.*